In the nearly two decades I have lived in Thailand, I have visited more than 50 provinces and run the gamut—sometimes it seemed more like the gauntlet—of travel experiences, from scuba diving and rock climbing to surviving a near-drowning experience in a kayak off the coast of Krabi, and from learning how to hunt for red ant egg nests (a delicacy in the northeast) to going trawling with Thai-Muslim fishermen down south. These experiences have underlined many of the stories and guidebooks I have written, as well as a non-fiction collection of features about the country's stranger side called *Bizarre Thailand: Tales of Crime, Sex and Black Magic*. For the last decade, I have been daylighting as the editor of some of the country's top travel magazines and contributing freelance features to magazines, newspapers and websites around the world. Also published by Tuttle in 2014 was my collection of prize-winning short stories, *The Phantom Lover and Other Thrilling Tales of Thailand*.

Jim Algie

Published by Tuttle Publishing, an imprint of Periplus Editions (HK) Ltd

www.tuttlepublishing.com

Copyright © 2012 Periplus Editions (HK) Ltd

ISBN: 978-0-8048-4210-5

Distributed by

North America, Latin America & Europe
Tuttle Publishing
364 Innovation Drive
North Clarendon, VT 05759-9436 U.S.A.
Tel: 1 (802) 773-8930
Fax: 1 (802) 773-6993
info@tuttlepublishing.com
www.tuttlepublishing.com

Japan
Tuttle Publishing
Yaekari Building, 3rd Floor
5-4-12 Osaki
Shinagawa-ku
Tokyo 141-0032
Tel: (81) 3 5437-0171
Fax: (81) 3 5437-0755
sales@tuttle.co.jp
www.tuttle.co.jp

Asia Pacific
Berkeley Books Pte. Ltd.
61 Tai Seng Avenue, #02-12
Singapore 534167
Tel: (65) 6280-1330
Fax: (65) 6280-6290
inquiries@periplus.com.sg
www.periplus.com

16 15 14   10 9 8 7 6 5 4 3 2
Printed in Singapore   1406CP

TUTTLE TRAVEL PACK

Thailand

Text by Jim Algie

TUTTLE Publishing

Tokyo | Rutland, Vermont | Singapore

The Thailand experience has something special for everyone!

There are hundreds of reasons why Thailand is the leader in repeat visitors and near the top in arrivals in Southeast Asia. First and foremost, the kingdom is a hodgepodge of influences that mix the region's crème de la crème in a savory, palatable and often wholly original way.

The country's northeast blends Lao and Khmer influences while Phuket's vintage architecture is Sino-Portuguese. The provinces and islands of the far south have a Malay vibe and linguistic flair while the Thai spirit is an Indian-influenced triumvirate of Buddhism, Brahminism and animism, fascinatingly juxtaposed against Bangkok's CBD of sky-rises that stand tall against their rivals from Hong Kong and Singapore. As in those cities, the ruling élite of the corporate world as well as the protagonists in the theater of politics mainly have Chinese bloodlines.

Another chapter in Thailand's tourism success story is that anyone plotting a trip or extended sojourn can swing from a frayed shoestring on the guesthouse circuit, go stratospheric with the high rollers relishing the region's most afford-able five-star facilities or navigate a truce between those extremes.

Bring the whole family or just your drinking buddies for a beachside bender. Go wild in the jungle or head out on a honeymoon after getting married on elephant back at a northern-style wedding. Come on business and stay for leisure. Book a healthy holiday at a detox/spa resort or let Dionysus be your tour guide on a wine-tasting trip through the new "Tuscany of Thailand".

Toss in ingredients like hospitable locals, solid infrastructure, safety and security, season with a benign climate that offers wildly differing environs, from limestone mountains to mangrove forests, from tropical beaches to impeccable rainforests, and Thailand is your all-in-one/whatever-you-want getaway.

This book is a distillation of my nearly two decades of living in the kingdom, a compendium of travels in 2013, and updates in 2014.

The modus operandi is concision. After all, lugging your baggage around under a mind-broiling sun can be arduous enough without adding a cinder block of a guidebook filled with all sorts of extraneous details.

At the same time, the tiny bytes of information and fingernail-sized photo-graphs on a smart phone cannot possibly do justice to an 11th-century Khmer ruin. The *Tuttle Travel Pack Thailand* occupies a Buddhist-style middle ground between these two extremes. I hope you enjoy the ride—and the *yin* and *yang* counterbalances.

CONTENTS

Thailand **Overview**

Thais refer to the country's shape as an "axe", the long handle formed by the Kra Isthmus with the Gulf of Thailand on one side and the Andaman Sea on the other. On the western flank is Myanmar, with Cambodia and Laos to the east. The head of the axe is serrated by the mountains of the "Golden Triangle" where Vietnam, Laos, Thailand and Myanmar merge.

Occupying a total of 514,000 square kilometers, Thailand is twice the size of England. It has six regions. The mountainous highlands of the north are home to many of the country's hilltribe minorities. This region is irrigated by the Wang, Ping, Yom and Nan Rivers, which are tributaries of the mighty, long Chao Phaya River that also bisects Bangkok. In the northeast is the Khorat Plateau of deciduous and evergreen forests. The central plains, known as the country's "rice bowl", are endowed with fecund farmlands. And extending into Cambodia are the Southeast Uplands that consist of moist evergreen forest. In contrast, the Tenasserim Hills, covered with semi-evergreen forests at higher altitudes, run alongside the border with Burma all the way down to the Kra Isthmus in the south.

In the multi-millennium-spanning epic that is Thai history, many ethnic groups—the Tai, Mons, Khmers, Indians and Europeans—have all contributed substantial chapters to this ongoing saga. From Southern China came the Tai people around AD 1100. From the Mons and Khmers came major advancements in language, art and architecture. From India came Buddhism. And from the Chinese immigrants came commercial acumen and family-first values.

The arrival of Buddhist missionaries from India around the second or third century BC is nebulous. More certain is that Buddhism began to spread during the Dvaravati period (6th–13th centuries AD), a loose configuration of city-states.

As in most of Southeast Asia, Theravada Buddhism is the kingdom's main form of spiritual solace (though it's been influenced by so many different strains of Brahmanism, Hinduism, shamanism and animism that it's almost a religion unto itself). Theravadan Buddhists pride themselves on a fundamentalist interpretation of the canon. Many of the loan words from Sanskrit and Pali, which defined the Buddhist scriptures, then became the linguistic roots of the tonal Thai tongue.

Smaller groups of Christians, Hindus, Taoists, Sikhs and Muslims coexist in relative peace except for the three south-

ern provinces abutting Malaysia (Yala, Pattani and Narathiwat) where a spate of bombings and beheadings has left a trail of murder and carnage since 2004.

One major reason why Thailand, alone in all of Indochina, managed to stave off colonization by European powers is that the country is so adept at adopting and assimilating foreign cultures. Since the Ayutthaya period (1351–1767), when foreign traders, missionaries and desperados first descended en masse in the 15th and 16th centuries, the country has displayed a famously tolerant attitude towards other nationalities, which has benefited tourism greatly and changed very little over the centuries.

Arguably no single person has had more of an impact on contemporary Thailand than King Rama V, who reigned from 1868 to 1910. In the late 19th century when he became the first Siamese monarch to visit Europe, he brought back with him a taste for Western-style suits, cigars and bowler hats, along with ideas to modernize the country by building roads and hospitals and abolishing slavery. His former palace, the Wimanmek Mansion, shows a willingness to counterpoint Western styles with Siamese iconography: the upholstered chairs in the world's largest golden teakwood mansion are ornamented with the gilded heads of the "serpent king" of Buddhist lore.

Contemporary Thai pop culture is as globalized, materialistic and mall-spawned as anywhere else in the developed world, with the influences of Korean and British pop, Japanese *manga*, and Hollywood and MTV hip-hop largely ensuring that classical Thai culture (the dances, masked dramas and trebly orchestras) plays second fiddle and is largely relegated to providing tourist entertainment and sporadic shows in the bigger urban areas like Bangkok.

But the portraits of King Rama V, which predominate in homes, offices, nightclubs, restaurants and even massage parlors, which are still worshipped as totems of the monarch who became a messiah from beyond the grave, go to show that beneath the globalized façade is a very Thai soul.

Thailand's
STORIED PAST

The founding of the Sukhothai ("Dawn of Happiness") kingdom in 1238, after the expulsion of Khmer forces, was truly the dawning of a new era in the country's history. Of all the kingdom's rulers, King Ramkhamhaeng (1275–1317) is one of the most legendary. He made Theravada Buddhism the main religion and, using Mon, Khmer and south India models, created the first Thai alphabet.

Under his rule, trade routes were established through much of Asia, and the arts blossomed. King Ramkhamhaeng (a long road in Bangkok is named after him) also gave his blessing to the formation of the northern Thai kingdom known

as Lanna ("A Million Ricefields") in 1296, which was overrun by Burmese hordes in 1558. During the Sukhothai period, such still-running festivals as Loy Krathong, where tiny floats adorned with flowers and candles are floated on the waterways, also began.

For more than four centuries (beginning in 1350), and through 34 reigns, the kingdom of Ayutthaya prospered until it finally went down in flames — torched and vanquished by the Burmese in 1767. During its heyday, this island was the richest port in the region. From the chronicles written by European traders, missionaries and diplomats, the city, and its royal court and golden Buddha images, made London and Paris seem drab by comparison.

The war hero who eventually drove the Burmese out of Ayutthaya, and then moved the new Siamese capital to Thonburi, had himself crowned as King Taksin. Having to continually fight off the Burmese and modify the country's political system took its toll on his mental health — to the point where he thought himself to be a Buddha-like figure, even if his violent behavior proved the opposite. He was forced to abdicate the throne in 1782. Later, fearing reprisals on his part, a group of generals stuffed him in a sack and pummeled him to death with sandalwood clubs, because royal blood cannot touch the earth.

The Rattanakosin period was a tumultuous time that saw the capital moved across the banks of the Chao Phraya River to Bangkok, and the coronation of the first king of the Chakri dynasty.

In 1932, a coup d'état (sans bloodletting), led to the development of a constitutional monarchy. Six years later, the name of the country was changed from Siam to Thailand. During World War II, the Japanese occupied parts of Thailand, perpetuating the atrocities involved with the construction of the infamous "Death Railway".

In 1946, a young monarch named Ananda Mahidol ascended the throne only to be shot dead a year later by a killer who has escaped detection. Next in line to the throne was his brother, Bhumibol Adulyadej, who became the world's longest reigning monarch in 1988. In 2011, there were countrywide tributes and events to mark the auspicious occasion of his 84th birthday.

After World War II, Thailand was ruled by a series of military strongmen who brooked no political opposition for the next few decades. Finally, in 1973, great masses of students began protesting for a real constitution and an end to dictatorships. A non-violent demonstration in October of that year turned the grounds of Thammasat University into a killing field when soldiers stormed in to break up the protest. The bloodbath in October of 1976 was considerably worse. These atrocities came full circle in 1992 during the "Black May" crisis, and once again during the "red shirt" protests on the streets of Bangkok in 2010 that left at least 91 people dead and thousands injured.

Much of Thailand's modern history has been scarred by political infighting and tainted with cases of corruption. After a series of short-lived governments following the coup that ousted Prime Minister Thaksin Shinawatra in 2006, the country's political situation remains shaky, even if it does have the second largest economy in Southeast Asia, and remains the undisputed leader in tourism.

Tuttle Travel Pack Thailand
HOW TO USE THIS BOOK

One thing that separates the Tuttle series of Travel Packs from the competition is that they are all written by insiders and expatriates with their fingers on the jugular of what makes a destination pulse.

What's more, the small size (easy to stick in a purse or back pocket) makes them portable companions, suitable for the repeat visitor or the first-timer. The format is a model of simplicity. At the front, you'll find all the background you need to enjoy Thailand, its rainbow of races, its tolerant and sometimes turbulent history, Buddhist underpinnings, regal lineage and diverse topography.

In Part 1, we cherry pick the can't-miss highlights of the country, from visiting the time capsule of Ayutthaya, the World Heritage Site only 90 minutes from Bangkok, to a night at the Muay Thai fights, navigating the Byzantine bazaar that is the Weekend Market, to sea kayaking Phang-nga Bay studded by 100-meter-high limestone karsts, and drinking in the neon-splashed nightscape from Bangkok's best rooftop bar.

In Part 2, we provide you with some overviews and sample itineraries to explore different parts of the country. In the central region, you can visit the country's oldest national park, Khao Yai, a small city overrun by monkeys (Lopburi) and the UNESCO-listed World Heritage Site of Ayutthaya.

Up north, you can explore the country's most famous treasure chest of antiques and new wave artworks, Chiang Mai, with its Night Bazaar, archaic temples and super cool boutique hotels, then head for the great green hills on a trek.

Down south, any visitor must avail themselves of the impeccable beaches, turquoise seas, seafood restaurants freshened with sea breezes and the many water sports available on Phuket, Ko Samui, Ko Lipe and other smaller islands, where your castaway fantasies become reality. We also let you in on some travel trade secrets about the new greenbelt of eco-tourism and green resorts that has sprouted in the North Andaman around Khao Lak.

In Part 3, our author on the inside puts forth his recommendations for the country's best hotels, spas, temples, shows, boutiques and restaurants.

For the final section, we give you the lowdown on everything from visas and tipping to cell phones, shipping, helpful phone numbers, emergency advice and transport information to smooth out a few speed bumps that may trip you up.

While all information is correct at time of print, make sure to call ahead or check the website of any venues listed in this book. In the travel business, here today, bankrupt tomorrow, is an irksome home truth.

As such, the publisher cannot accept responsibility for any errors that may be contained within the Travel Pack.

CHAPTER 1
THAILAND'S
'Must See' Sights

Without obtaining God-like powers of omniscience, it would be impossible to nail down a best-of-the-best list in an exact running order that would be valid 24/7, 365 days a year. These are recommendations, signposts if you will, to point you in the right direction. The real thrill of discovery is turning off your GPS system, taking a left when the guidebook says right and venturing out on your own. Just outside the comfort zones of these recommendations, the real adventure begins.

1 The Grand Palace, Bangkok
2 Phuket's Mai Khao Bay
3 Ayutthaya's Golden Heydays
4 Massage at Wat Pho Temple
5 Chatuchak Weekend Market
6 High Tea at the Oriental Hotel
7 Phang-nga Bay, Phuket
8 The Elephant Conservation Center
9 Wat Phrathai Doi Suthep
10 A Muay Thai Boxing Match
11 A Long-tail Boat Ride in Bangkok
12 Bangkok's Red Sky Rooftop Bar
13 Khao Yai National Park
14 Diving at Ko Tao Island
15 Chiang Mai's Wat Chiang Man
16 Bangkok's Infamous Patpong Road
17 Lopburi Monkey Temples
18 A Thai Village Homestay
19 Ko Samui's Wellness Retreats
20 Dining at Soi 38, Sukhumvit
21 Sunset at Promthep Cape

Making the Most of Your Visit

On the road, few things are more exasperating than racing around trying to fill a pie-in-the-sky itinerary only to be gridlocked at every stop. This woe can be exacerbated in Bangkok's traffic, in Chiang Mai with its notorious lack of public transport, and on Phuket where the so-called "tuk-tuk mafia" charge extortionate rates for short hops.

First of all, you'll need to decide on your mode of transport. Budget carriers now link most of the major destinations. Trains are cheap and buses plentiful, but both are slow.

Once you've arrived, cars and motorcycles are reasonably cheap to rent. The latter are considerably more dangerous and out of bounds in Bangkok, where the skytrain and subway have given a double bypass to some of the most traffic-clogged arteries. In the ancient cities of Ayutthaya and Sukhothai, renting a bicycle is the way to go, whereas in smaller hamlets like Lopburi, your feet are the perfect means of transport.

It's also best to balance out a sightseeing day with a variety of attractions so that you're not trudging through temple after temple or museum after museum.

Of elementary importance when drafting any itinerary is considering the seasons. During the sweltering season, for instance, from February through April, when the mercury can soar to the upper 30s on the Celsius scale, try to factor in some "air-con time" in malls and restaurants. The rainy season is often quite sunny, except for September (the wettest month of the year), but trekking or bird watching in national parks at this time of year can suck because of all the leeches. Conversely, the cool season from November through January is a great time for hiking and mountain biking, though be warned it can get down to zero Celsius at night in the mountain-studded north country. During the monsoon season, from May through October, there is no ferry service to the Similans National Marine Park, and it may be sporadic to some of the more remote islands like Ko Lipe.

Also remember to factor in some cultural peculiarities like opening hours. Because of some arcane law, the majority of national museums, and other such government repositories, are closed on Monday and Tuesday. Buddhist holidays can also put a spanner in the works of any journey, and the country's major festivals, such as the Thai New Near in mid-April, need to be taken into account. During the spectacularly grisly Vegetarian Festival on Phuket, for example, expect that rooms in the city of Phuket will be booked solid for months in advance.

The easiest way to come up with an itinerary is by breaking the country down into its four regions. After exploring Bangkok, discover the central region, with stopovers in Ayutthaya, Lopburi (both easily accessed by frequent and inexpensive trains) and Khao Yai National Park. If heading north, look at the big destinations, like Chiang Mai, Sukhothai, Pai and Chiang Rai, linked by low-cost flights. In the Gulf of Thailand, draft a travel plan that encompasses the major gateways and destinations, like Ko Samui, the Angthong National Marine Park, the scuba diving capital of Ko Tao and the hedonist's haven of Ko Phangan, home to the Full Moon Party. Once you've got the gateways sorted for transport, and a sketch of the bigger sights, it's much easier to connect the dots and home in on the smaller places and the roads less traveled.

1 The Grand Palace, Bangkok
Regal grandeur from the 18th century

The Grand Palace, with its majestic pagodas, giant-sized guardians, colorful murals and exquisitely wrought sculptures, was a bold attempt to equal the glories of the palace in the former royal capital of Ayutthaya. Extending over almost a million square meters and fortified by walls built in 1783, the palace, which adjoins the **Temple of the Emerald Buddha**, is Thailand's number one tourist attraction. The presence of tourists, however, has done little to diminish its grandeur, and many Thais still come to pay their respects and seek blessings, giving a dose of reality to this regally Buddhist fantasia, even if there are no monks quartered here.

After you buy your ticket and enter the complex, you see a seated hermit-cum-physician made out of bronze. King Rama III had this statue cast when he was restoring his residence and adding touches like flowerpots, stone seats and Chinese sculptures. Much of this restoration work was carried out in 1831 for Bangkok's 50th anniversary celebrations in 1832.

Walk past the two *yaksha* (gigantic demons with the tusks of wild boars) installed during the reign of King Rama II, and go up the stairs to the great gilt *chedi*, which is the tallest structure in the whole complex. This reliquary houses a piece of the Buddha's breastbone. The complex is renowned for containing the country's holiest of holies, the Emerald Buddha, a surprisingly small image.

The 178 refurbished murals that summarize the plot of *The Ramayana* are equally famous. (The Indian saga that is the wellspring for traditional Khmer dances, Thai masked dramas and Indonesian shadow plays is to Southeast Asian art and literature what Homer's *The Iliad* is to Western letters.)

At the entrance to the actual palace, two guardian demons stand sentry beside it. Like the Temple of the Emerald Buddha, this group of lavish buildings was constructed in 1782, and served as the official residence of the king until 1946. However, King Rama V was the last monarch to actually live here in the early 20th century.

Opening Times Daily 8.30 am–3.30 pm

Address Na Phra Lan Road, near Sanam Luang

Getting There Take the Chao Phraya River Express taxi to the Tha Chang Pier

Contact +66 (0)2 222 0094, +66 (0)2 222 6889

Admission Fee 400 baht

2 Phuket's Mai Khao Bay
Tropical splendor on Thailand's biggest island

Soaking up the sun and drinking in the tropical scenery of **Mai Khao Bay** on the northwest coast of Phuket is about as sublime as castaway dreams get. The island's longest stretch of sand (11 kilometers) makes for the archetypal getaway. All by yourself, save for the birds and hermit crabs, induces a Robinson Crusoe sense of solitude that is meditative. Suddenly, office politics seem trivial and personal woes go on vacation.

The deserted beach used to be a favorite haunt for the giant leatherback turtle which had waddled ashore to lay their eggs from time immemorial. But those numbers have dipped catastrophically in recent years.

Local authorities have responded by monitoring the nesting procedures closely and moving the eggs to special hatcheries, where the young can be released later.

The two most northern beaches on Phuket, Mai Khao and **Nai Yang**, form the blessedly undeveloped Sirinath National Park. Beware that the tides here, especially during the monsoon season, can be treacherous and riptides run rife.

In the vicinity are a few other distractions like the **Turtle Village** shopping complex. Here, the accent is mostly on smaller shops for arts and curios, upscale beachwear and a Jim Thompson outlet for Thai silk products.

A few five-star resorts, namely the Anantara and the JW Marriott, have also laid claim to some prime real estate. On the grounds of the West Sands Resort, the **Splash Jungle Water Park** provides a dash of Disney with an aquatic atmosphere and enough pools, rides and water slides to keep the most hyperactive of kids satisfied.

Even these intrusions are minimal. In the vast expanse of Mai Khao, affording from-there-to-infinity views of the sea and horizon, life is reduced to its most primordial elements: sea, sky, earth and shy sea creatures.

Opening Times 24/7. During the monsoon season from May to November, swimming can be perilous

Address Northwest part of island

Getting There Take the main road Highway 402, then look for the signs for Turtle Village

3 Ayutthaya
Golden heydays shine on

Once touted as the most glorious city in the world, **Ayutthaya** was both the nucleus and the soul of ancient Siam. Only 90 minutes north of Bangkok, the city straddles the crossroads of Southeast Asian history.

In AD 1350, the capital of a soon-to-be-formidable empire was founded by King Ramathibodi I. His ashes are interred in one of the three massive *chedi* at **Wat Pra Sri San Phet**, where the royal palace once stood. Constructed at the behest of Ramathibodi II to house the mortal dust of his father and brother, the *chedi* stand as monuments to filial devotion.

It's difficult to imagine how life was lived way back when cowrie shells were used as currency and people slept with machetes beside their beds, unless you see these slices of ancient Siamese life at the **Ayutthaya Historical Study Center** and the **Chao Phraya Sam Museum**. The latter also contains models of the city in its heyday, a Chinese junk, ceremonial swords and jewel-studded elephant trinkets.

The gold artifacts give off a few glimmers of Ayutthaya's legend among foreign traders and missionaries as an El Dorado or City of Gold. Discovered in the *prang* (a stubby Khmer-style tower) of **Wat Ratchaburana**, the treasures were untouched by the Burmese soldiers who razed, pillaged and left the city a smoldering cremation ground in 1767. They made off with so much gold, in fact, that Thai history books claim the streets were littered with glittering fragments of the metal.

Rent a bicycle to explore the historical park or see the ruins on the back of a lumbering elephant helmed by a mahout

in a costume of glimmering red and gold silk. Charter a long-tail boat over at the pier by the **Chandra Kasem Palace** (another museum with gold treasures) and explore the three rivers that form a natural moat around the city. En route there are stops at major temples like **Wat Phutthaisawan**, which has a large reclining Buddha image meant to symbolize his passage into nirvana.

From the river, you can also see a **monument to Queen Suriyothai**, the tragic 16th-century heroine who disguised herself as a man to ride out on the battlefield where her husband was facing off against the Burmese king in an elephant-back duel. She rode between them, sacrificing her life for her husband's, while creating a larger-than-death legend and the heroine of *Suriyothai*, the period piece from 2000 that remains Thailand's biggest blockbuster.

The rivers are particularly picturesque around dusk. Then, as the boat speeds towards them, the temples slowly rise out of the smoke-blue distance like little has changed in the past five centuries.

Opening Times Daily 6.00 am–6.00 pm

Address Ayutthaya Historical Park

Getting There Ayutthaya is 76 km north of Bangkok. Trains depart every hour from 4.20 am to 10 pm for 15 baht in third-class non-air con from Hua Lamphong Station, Bangkok

Contact Office of Ayutthaya Historical Park Tel: +66 (0)3 524 2501, +66 (0)3 524 4570

Admission Fee 30 baht

4 Massage at Wat Pho Temple
Get rubbed the right way at the country's first university

Famously described by some travelers as a "lazy person's yoga", Thai massage, like acupuncture using hands, elbows and feet instead of needles, helps to unblock the power lines of the body's natural grid of nerves and muscles to boost energy levels and keep people limber.

As attested to by some of the sculptures in Bangkok's **Wat Pho**, home to the most famous massage center and a nearby school, this healing art requires some circus-like contortions.

Dating back some 2,500 years to the time of the Buddha, Thai massage has more than a few similarities to yoga. Admittedly, the masseuse might touch on some sore spots. So it's best to tell them in advance about any physical problems you have or areas to avoid. At the same time, you should also tell them what kind of pressure to apply.

At the bottom end, there are little massage parlors all over the bigger tourist areas. They usually offer a full menu of treatments such as reflexology, oil massage and different strains such as Swedish and Balinese (both a lot more gentle than the Thai variety). In the upper range, the top hotels and resorts usually have their own spas offering different massages for about four to five times as much as the smaller places.

At the end of a long day of sightseeing, a good massage is just what the doctor ordered. Though a little painful at times, the end result is worth it for feeling rejuvenated and about five kilos lighter.

Some converts even sign up to take classes. Of these learning centers, the most renowned is the **Wat Pho School of Traditional Medicine and Massage**, where a beginner's class lasts 30 hours, six hours a day for five days straight, including plenty of hands-on practice.

Opening Times Daily 8 am–5 pm

Address 248 Thanon Thai Wang, entrance on Chetupon Road

Getting There Take river taxi to Tha Chang Pier

Contact +66 (0)2 281 2831

Admission Fee 50 baht

5 Chatuchak Weekend Market
Behemoth of a bazaar for serial shoppers

The **Chatuchak Weekend Market** in Bangkok is a world unto itself. Covering the area of a village, but with the transient population of a small city, "JJ" (as Thais call it as it is pronounced "Jatujak") offers everything from second-hand clothes to first-class artworks, and old-fashioned hilltribe regalia to new school furniture, besides a laundry list of other items, like exotic pets for the politically suspect, PVC handbags decorated with dried flowers, household decorations and Vietnam War-era memorabilia.

Navigating this sweltering maze of 15,000 vendors can overload and short-circuit both your senses and patience. For a personal compass, the handiest tool is the Nancy Chandler Map of Bangkok with a large section on the world's most gigantic weekend market. At the head offices near the back of the market, free maps are available. They are okay to get your bearings but don't provide a lot of information about which goods are where.

Better still are the billboards located around the market, mapping out the many lanes and sign posting the sections. Using the huge clock tower in the middle of Chatuchak as a signpost also helps to stave off disorientation.

The majority of the market is dedicated to clothes and footwear. The stalls for new clothes are found in Section 10 and in the even-numbered sections that follow it all the way up to 20. Whether it's knock-off designer jeans or the latest trainers, affordable T-shirts or tropical-hued beachwear, this area is well suited to all your clothing needs.

Chatuchak is renowned for its motley collection of arts and handicrafts, ranging from the ridiculous (baseball caps made out of beer cans) to the sublime (Thai silk). In particular, Sections 24 and 26 are laden with the full spectrum of wood carvings, bronzeware, lacquerware, purses woven from vines, and the local ceramics known as *benjarong* for the combination of five colors that enrich these miniature tea sets, bowls and vases.

Perhaps the penultimate rule in this jungle of consumerism is to make your purchase then and there, because you might not find your way back to that little shop again.

Opening Times Weekends 8 am–6 pm

Address Kamphaeng Phet 3 Road

Getting There Take skytrain to Mor Chit Station or subway to Kamphaengphet Station

Admission Fee Free

6 High Tea at the Oriental Hotel
It's every moneyed traveler's cup of tea

To fully revel in Bangkok's old world charm, the **Mandarin Oriental** serves high tea in the **Author's Lounge**, full of period furniture and gingerbread fretwork, with all the delectable trimmings like fresh strawberries and scones.

The long list of celebrity guests, such as Nicholas Cage, Mick Jagger and Sir Peter Ustinov, are proof of its ascendancy into the stratosphere of hotels which, given its humble origins, makes it seem all the more remarkable.

Back in the 19th century, the hotel provided lodgings and a bar for seamen at a time when Bangkok had no other such facilities and only one decent thoroughfare (the nearby New Road), where gas street lamps were finally installed in 1866. Less than two decades later, Joseph Conrad, still a sailor and not yet the author of famous works like *Heart of Darkness*, hung out at the bar.

In subsequent decades, the hotel's poetic décor and riverside setting shanghaied the imaginations and livers of other celebrity writers of the likes of Somerset Maugham and Noel Coward, who have suites named after them in the Author's Wing—the oldest part of the hotel—where high tea is served with crisp linen amidst white rattan furniture and a library of classics.

Before the end of the 19th century, the Oriental had become the first luxury hotel in the country. Opulence still reigns at the hotel, and many visitors stop by for a glimpse, a cup of tea or a meal at one of the seven superb restaurants, such as the seafood specialist **Lord Jim's** (named after Conrad's novel).

Across the river at the hotel's **Sala Rim Naam**, guests can savor classical Thai dances and performances, while gorging themselves on a set menu of local staples, or get a spa treatment at the **Oriental Ayurvedic Penthouse**. For a double shot of jazz with a chaser of blues, the hotel's legendary **Bamboo Bar** is just the place for thirsty ears.

Opening Times Daily noon–6 pm

Address 48 Oriental Avenue

Getting There Catch skytrain to Saphan Taksin Station and five-minute taxi ride from there

Contact +66 (0)2 659 9000; mobkk-enquiry@mohg.com

7 Phang-nga Bay, Phuket
The ninth wonder of the water world

Take a survey of any 10 wayfarers cruising around the coasts of Krabi and Phuket on what their favorite day-trip is and the smart money is on sea canoeing in **Phang-nga Bay**. One of the world's most incredibly natural marvels, the bay is studded with some 40 sheer limestone karsts that rise vertically out of the sea for hundreds of meters. It's like a tropical seascape envisioned by Salvador Dali.

Nature's exclamation marks, the limestone cliffs are pocked with sea caves, collapsed cave systems open to the sky and surrounded by limestone walls, that are only accessible during daylight's low tide. The local "paddle guides" have to navigate their rubber canoes through chinks in the cliffs so narrow that both navigator and daytripper have to lie flat on their backs.

Miraculously, the caves open into lagoons with water that looks like melted-down emeralds surrounded by ramparts of limestone. Equally as photogenic are the looks of awe on the faces of the other visitors as they catch their first glimpses of these Jurassic flashbacks.

Monitor lizards, monkeys, sea eagles and black kingfishers are known to make cameos. Some lagoons are fringed with mangrove forests. The roots of these trees grow right out of the water.

Another passageway through the rocks is known as the "Bat Cave". When the guide shines a pocket torch on the ceiling of the cave, where thousands and thousands of bats hang as if in suspended animation, the name is a dead giveaway.

Many daytrips include a stopover at the overrated and underwhelming **James Bond Island** (Ko Ta-pu or "Nail Island")—a tourist trap full of tacky souvenirs—lunch on board the boat, as well as some sessions of swimming and sun-basking on uninhabited islands.

Opening Times 24/7 but daylight visits and guides recommended

Address East coast of the island

Getting There Take a full-day tour from Phuket for US$40–100, including lunch, water, snacks, etc. For a pricier alternative, try John Gray's Sea Canoe. The veteran tour operator offers the "Hong by Starlight" package—'hong is sea cave'—priced at around US$130 per person

8 The Elephant Conservation Center
On the shoulders of giants

As the former mascot of Siam's flag, and revered by many Thais as the most regal of beasts, the elephant still occupies a prominent place in local history and folklore, even as the herds thin and the mythology wanes. On most of the major islands, like Ko Samui, Phuket and Ko Chang, and especially in the northern part of the country, riding an elephant is a rite of passage for first-time visitors to the kingdom.

For festivals, the **Elephant Roundup**, where they reenact famous battles fought from the backs of pachyderms, lumbers into action every November in Surin (the province that is home to the most creatures and mahouts).

For those animal lovers who really want to experience the life of an elephant handler and learn how to "drive" the world's largest land animal, the **Elephant Conservation Center** in the province of Lampang is a good choice. Many visitors opt for the three-day course. Expect to go "rustic" and live, eat and hang out with the real mahouts. Also expect to have your own elephant assigned to you for the duration of the course. Come sundown, when the elephants are taken to bathe in the river, it turns into a free-for-all water fight as the tuskers use their trunks like fire hoses.

Most guests at the center wax rhapsodic about the authentic Thai fare served at the homestay, though they also grumble about the roosters crowing all night and the necessity of bringing a good pair of earplugs.

Originally set up as a hospital for wounded pachyderms back in 1992 — when a young female had her leg blown off by a landmine along the Thai-Burma border where she was illegally employed to haul logs — the Elephant Conservation Center is helping to bestow some dignity upon a vanishing breed rapidly being reduced to a clown show and circus act.

Opening Times Daily 8 am–6 pm

Address 28-29 Lampang-Chiang Mai Highway

Getting There From Bangkok catch the train at Hualamphong Station bound for Chiang Mai and get off in Lampang. The trip takes 10–12 hours. Bangkok Airways has one flight per day from Suvannabhumi International Airport to Lampang.

Contact +66 (0)5 424 7875, www.changthai.com

Admission Fee Various programmes from one-day visits to 10-day-long mahout training programmes. See website for prices.

9 Wat Phrathai Doi Suthep
Holy mountain stands tall

Wat Phrathai Doi Suthep is the pinnacle of northern spirituality: a mountaintop temple outside Chiang Mai with a cornerstone erected on fantastical tales about a monk and a Buddha relic and a white elephant who died up here. Whatever one believes, the golden *chedi* gilded with sunlight, the shrine to the sacred tusker, and the balustrades made from the snake-like body and crested head of Phaya Nak ("The Serpent King") certainly do look otherworldly.

The view of the city from on high, some 1,066 meters above sea level, is also fit for a deity. From the road, the not so fleet of foot can skip the 300 steps by riding the cable car up to the temple.

The complex is a fanciful confection of Buddhist and Hindu elements, with the fairytale whimsy and those brightly hued colors that appeal to Thai aesthetics. With a history dating back more than six centuries, the temple is hugely popular with both locals and tourists. For all that, Doi Suthep (it's often referred to by the name of the mountain it crowns) is a real temple with genuine supplicants and monks. There is also a model of the "Emerald Buddha" on hand that inspires veneration.

Standing almost 1,830 meters high, the mountain and its sister peak are part of the **Doi Suthep-Doi Pui National Park**. It's also one of the kingdom's best bird watching areas. Near the temple are Hmong hilltribe villages.

As the Thai saying goes, "If you haven't eaten *khao soy* (a spicy northern-style curry with crispy noodles) or seen the view from atop Doi Suthep, then you haven't been to Chiang Mai."

Opening Times Daily 6 am–8 pm

Address Km 14, Srivichai Road

Getting There By car or tuk-tuk the temple complex is 30 minutes from the center of Chiang Mai

Contact +66 (0)5 324 8604

Admission Fee Climb the 300 steps for free or take the tram for 30 baht.

10 A Muay Thai Boxing Match
Punchy entertainment for the whole family

Muay Thai is the most artistic and mystical way for two men to beat the snot out of each other. As the two fighters step into the ring of the new **Lumpinee Boxing Stadium**, opened in 2014 on Bangkok's Ram Intra Road—the sport's Mount Olympus for regular clashes of the Thai titans—they are both wearing garlands of marigolds around their necks and colorful headbands. After removing their silky robes, the two barefooted boxers walk around the ring, stopping to pray in each corner to the guardian spirit of the ring.

Then live classical music composed of two drummers hand-pummelling their instruments, another man clinking finger cymbals together, and a Thai-style oboist playing melodies serpentine enough to charm a cobra, kicks in. The two boxers begin dancing around the ring. Their slow fluid movements ape the graceful movements of Thai classical dance. Occasionally, they both kneel down, touching their foreheads to the mat in obeisance to their coaches. After the two fighters and their coaches pray together

for a minute in both corners of the ring, their mentors then remove the boxers' garlands and headbands.

In a martial art that flagrantly mixes the sacred with the profane, the men in the crowd make gestures and wagers on the outcome of the match before each fight begins.

Make no bones about it, Muay Thai is brutal. Each of the 10 matches on a fight card, which begins in the early evening and lasts until 10.30 pm, is filled with punches to the head, elbows to the jaw, knees to the rib cage and vicious kicks to the throat, chest and calves.

For the historical record, the origins of Thai-style kickboxing date back more than a 1,000 years, when a manual on warfare called the *Chupasart* instructed Tai warriors how to do battle with various weapons. When applying these techniques to hand-to-hand combat, the fists became the spear tips, the elbows and knees the battle axes, and the shin bones turned into the staff of the pike to both block and strike.

In 2014, the Asiatique riverside bazaar added a nightly extravaganza called "Muay Thai Live" which is an entertaining history of the sport and a well-choreographed martial arts spectacle.

Opening Times 6–10pm, Tuesday, Friday and Saturday at Lumpinee Boxing Stadium and Monday, Wednesday, Thursday, Sunday at Ratchadamnoen Boxing Stadium, which is near Khaosan Road and Democracy Monument.

Address Lumpinee Boxing Stadium, Anusawaree, No. 6, Ramintra Road, Ratchadamnoen Stadium at 1 Ratchadamnoen Nok

Admission Fee 1,000, 1,500 and 2,000 baht

11 A Long-tail Boat Ride in Bangkok
Cultural immersion on an epically affordable scale

The canals of Bangkok Yai and Bangkok Noi ("big" and "little" respectively) are capillaries that branch off from the main jugular vein of the Chao Phraya River. Twisting through the Thonburi side of the capital they are timelines flowing back through the centuries when Bangkok was called the "Venice of the East."

Chartering a long-tail boat to explore them could almost be classified as a "thrill sport". The prow, laden with garlands to appease the Water Goddess, spears through the waves while the boatman at the back of the vessel steers it with a rudder connected to a big, noisy, diesel-spewing engine, which moves fast enough to have spawned a chase scene in the 1974 James Bond vehicle *The Man with the Golden Gun.*

The canals are awash with traditional sights. Children use them as ad hoc swimming pools. Women use them to wash clothes. Vendors ferry fruits and vegetables to fresh markets. Families gather under the wooden pavilions in front of their houses that hover just above the waterline. And teenage boys play *takraw* —a kind of Southeast Asian volleyball played with a rattan ball manipulated by the feet, elbows and shoulders —on the grounds of Buddhist temples bordering the river.

Most of these long-tail tours, departing from the bigger piers such as Ta Chang, near the Grand Palace, will include stopovers at the more impressive sights, such as the **Royal Barges Museum** and the **Temple of Dawn (Wat Arun)**.

The saltier and more intrepid souls will, however, want to catch the river taxi to the end of the northern line in Nonthaburi, about an hour away. There, you can charter another long-tail boat to the tiny island of **Ko Kret**. Home to some 4,000, mostly ethnic Mon inhabitants, this enclave of artisans and spinners of pottery has no main roads or hotels. In an hour or so you can circumnavigate it by foot. Nearby is **Khlong Om**, another flashback of Bangkok's Venetian past with a Siamese slant, reflected in its riverside temples and Thai-style houses.

Opening Times Khlong tours run from around 9 am–5 pm from many of the major piers in Bangkok. Bargaining is necessary but expect to pay around 2,000 baht for a long-tail boat or around 500 baht per person.

Fee Around 500 baht per person

12 Bangkok's Red Sky Rooftop Bar
Rising above the mayhem of the metropolis

Even taking into account the high standards set by Bangkok's rooftop restaurants, **Red Sky** rises above much of the competition. At first glance, the roof of the **Centara Grand** hotel looks like it's sprouted a gigantic lotus blossom that slowly changes hues and has an illuminated stem running down the side of the building.

Inside, there are indoor areas with live jazz, an outdoor bar and area to chill out with the evening breeze, and another watering hole up above with 360-degree views of the "Big Mango" from 55 stories above the swarming streets. The wine list is so extensive that they have a special "glass elevator" to traverse the wine loft for that elusive bottle, while the Martini Bar whips up some of the city's most originally inebriating concoctions (passion fruit is the house specialty).

Meanwhile, the pan-European menu, with Asia Pacific accents, will take your taste buds on a journey of gastronomy through Italy, France, Tasmania, New Zealand and the US. Their signature dish, the two-story "Red Sky Surf & Turf

Tower", starring Alaskan king crab, giant Andaman shrimps, wagyu rib eye and grilled Maine lobster, is a work of sculptural art where style marries savory substance (a motif carried off with aplomb throughout the different bars and restaurants).

To be fair, Bangkok's glitzy hotels and high-rises have sprouted a number of crowning achievements in recent years, such as Sirocco on the **State Tower** as well as the Vertigo Grill and Moon Bar top hatting the **Banyan Tree**. All are sublime choices for a rendezvous with friends, rekindling old flames or sparking new romances, though visitors should be aware that the prices are as stratospheric as the views.

Opening Times Daily 6 pm–1 am

Address 999/99 Rama I Road, 55th floor of the Centara Grand

Getting There Short walk from Siam Square Skytrain Station

Contact +66 (0)2 100 1234

Admission Fee Drinks and dishes are as steeply priced as the view

13 Khao Yai National Park
Go wild and glut yourself on greenery

Khao Yai, the country's oldest and biggest national park, is an Asian safari park that stretches across four provinces and 2,000 kilometers. Sometimes sambar deer graze in the parking lot. Bull elephants lock tusks on salt licks and, in one fell swoop of an outing, trekkers can spot rhinoceros hornbills, whooping gibbons and Asiatic jackals.

Some 70 percent of these environs are made up of moist evergreen forest. Named after the park's centerpiece, Khao Yai ("Big Mountain"), the roads twist and wind around photogenic foothills. Though around one million people visit the park every year—most are weekend picnickers from Bangkok, less than three hours away—it still shelters and succors some 350 different species of bird, like the Siamese fireback pheasant, and around 80 different mammals, from Asiatic black bears to Malayan porcupines.

The lords of these jungles are the elephants. At least a hundred wild ones live within the confines of the park. Oftentimes they'll be spotted on the roads or heard trumpeting in the distance.

The park is also rich in orchid species. For its phenomenal bounty of flora and fauna, Khao Yai was granted UNESCO World Heritage Site Status in 2005.

One of the best things about the park

is that it can be done on so many different levels, from five-star opulence to guesthouse grittiness. You can go on one of the guided tours led by the resorts lining the main road near the town of Pak Chong or wander around on your own. Any jaunt can be combined with an array of other options, like wine tasting tours of the local vineries or making a pit stop at the area and shopping plaza called "Little Tuscany".

Opening Times Daily 6 am–9 pm

Address The park is spread over Nakhon Ratchasima, Saraburi, Prachinburi and Nakhon Nayok provinces

Getting There Those in need of accommodation stay in the town of Pak Chong in Nakhon Ratchasima province, while those coming on daytrips use the park's south entrance, which is about 13 km north of Prachinburi. Head north on the roundabout on Road 3077.

Contact The Visitor's Center is at (025) 620 760 and it's open from 8.30–4.30 pm. Make sure to hire a guide here if you plan to do any serious hiking. In case you get lost, the local tourist police office is at (044) 341 7778. Also note that because of all the mountains, mobile phone service can be sketchy.

Admission Fee 400 baht for foreigners

14 Diving at Ko Tao Island
Into the deep blue yonder for a psychedelic adventure

Perhaps Arthur C Clarke, the fabled author of *2001: A Space Odyssey* described scuba diving in the most memorable terms, as the closest you'll ever get to feeling as weightless as an astronaut floating in outer space.

Thailand is overflowing with reefs, pinnacles and wrecks for divers to chart and explore. If you're yet to get your fins wet, then **Ko Tao** ("Turtle Island"), located near the western shore of the Gulf of Thailand, is the place to get your license. In fact, more divers get certified on this island (only 21 square kilometers) than anywhere else in Southeast Asia.

Because of the glut of dive shops on the island, the prices are competitive.

Most shops offer the world's number one course for aspiring aquanauts, the PADI Open Water Dive Course. You will need to set aside three or four days to earn this globally recognized certificate. Each course combines classroom learning with lessons in a swimming pool or in shallow water off the beach, a final written exam and a proper plunge to around 15 meters.

Thanks to Ko Tao's abundance of shallow reefs and mostly gentle currents, newbies will not be out of their depth. Admittedly, learning to breath through the scuba device—and especially hearing your own breath rattling like the raspy voice of Darth Vader—takes some getting used to, but the rewards are well worth the risk.

Imagine if Alice fell through the looking glass and ended up in the world's biggest aquarium, swimming with exotic creatures like angelfish, moray eels, black tip reef sharks, and even the world's biggest fish, the humongous whale shark, while surrounded by brain coral, purple sea anemones and psychedelic reefs (the so-called "rainforests of the sea"), it's easy to see why diving is the best and most potent legal high on the market.

The island also offers some hiking, rock climbing and bouldering on granite boulder strewn beaches. Ko Tao is also a mecca for game fishermen on a budget.

Getting There Take a ferry from Surat Thani (4 hours), Chumpon (2–3 hours), Ko Samui (2.5 hours or Ko Ph Ngan (1 hour) to Ban Mae Haad. Prices depend on type of boat.

15 Chiang Mai's Wat Chiang Man
Get to the spiritual heart of Lanna culture

For a sampler of the northern capital's archaic and contemporary sides, the Old City is the nucleus. To set the historic scene, it's surrounded by red ramparts with four gates, a moat and fountains all lit up at night. Within these hallowed walls is the city's oldest temple, **Wat Chiang Man**. Its history stretches back to AD 1297 when King Mengrai founded this bastion of Lanna culture. The oldest part of the temple, a golden *chedi* propped up by a base of 15 brick and stucco elephants, is fit to be framed.

Another bulwark of the city's Buddhist-leaning spirituality is **Wat Phra Singh**. It may date back to AD 1345, but with all the monks and supplicants around, the temple still plays a pivotal part in the present.

Those who mock "temple huggers" as an effete breed of politically correct travelers will find plenty of other distractions in the Old City, from pubs and cafes to specialist bars and restaurants galore.

Prominent among the temple alternatives is the **Chiang Mai City Arts and Cultural Center**. Set within the confines of a beautiful old building, the center has rooms for permanent and temporary exhibitions, exhibitions on the city's prehistoric past, audiovisual displays on the hilltribes and, from time to time, cultural jamborees of the old-school variety.

Out in front is the **Three Kings Monument** composed of a holy trinity of god-like monarchs: Mengrai and Ramkhamhaeng of Sukhothai and Ngam Muang of Phayao.

As a city that has reinvented itself

many times over, Chiang Mai's latest reincarnation is as a hub of art and design. On and off the bigger streets and little lanes of the Old City, that word-of-mouth hype is made manifest in all the little shops and stalls specializing in cool curios and funky fashions.

The best time to sample the area is on Sundays when the main byway of Rachadamnoen Road is turned into a serene street party for shoppers, foodies and families replete with musicians, dancers and plenty of bonhomie.

Opening Times Daily 8 am–5 pm

Address Ratchaphakhinai Road near intersection with Si Phum Road

Getting There Situated in the old walled part of town, the temple is within walking distance of the Chang Phuak Gate

Contact +66 (0)5 321 3170

Admission Fee Free

16 Bangkok's Infamous Patpong Road
One night in Bangkok makes a hard man humble

Yes, it's noisy, gaudy, saucy, silly and a bit sleazy at times, but when in Asia's neon Rome do as the neo-Romans would and head for a stroll down the lanes of **Patpong 1 and 2**. By day it's as if the street is sleeping off a hangover, but at night it's back on another bender, doing a roaring trade in the world's oldest profession, which revolves around the chrome poles of go-go bars, while the stalls in the night market sell knock-off jeans, DVDs and Buddhist bric-a-brac. There are no bargains here; everything is overpriced.

At ground level, on each side of Patpong 1, are very similar go-go bars, with a razzle-dazzle of neon and a cacophony of processed-cheese techno. Upstairs on Patpong 1 are bars with much racier shows. Some of them have been known to slip customers with a huge bill for only a drink or two, necessitating a visit to the Tourist Police, who keep a van positioned at the end of Patpong 1. Be very wary of the upstairs bars and the touts on the street promoting their wares.

Patpong 2 is not such a hard sell; it's got more beer bars, restaurants and cocktail lounges with hostesses.

Both of the roads are named after the Hainanese immigrants with the surname of Patpongpanich, who bought the thoroughfare in 1946 and still own it. In the late 1960s and early 1970s, it first became notorious when go-go bars opened up to service the American troops on R&R during the Vietnam War. But it was not until the late 1980s that the night market got up and vending.

For years now, Patpong's reputation as the city's tenderloin for tourists is slowly being outstripped and upstaged by Nana Plaza and Soi Cowboy, although neither of those red-light areas have a night bazaar or the diversity of entertainment.

Opening Times Daily 7 pm–1 am

Address Patpong Road 1 and 2 stretch between Silom and Surawong

Getting There Take the skytrain to Sala Daeng Station and it's a five-minute walk south of there

Admission Fee Free

17 Lopburi Monkey Temples
Mayhem and mythology in the legendary town of Lopburi

It sounds too weird to be true. No, but really, there is a small city in central Thailand, about 150 kilometers northeast of Bangkok, where thousands of monkeys live on rooftops and inside a couple of Angkor-era shrines. The creatures swing from power poles, try to pickpocket tourists and scamper down the street.

Wait. It gets weirder. Locals see them as incarnations of Hanuman, the monkey god of Hinduism, so they generally treat them with respect.

If that still isn't odd enough for you, these macaques are as territorial as gang-bangers from New York. The monkeys are separated into three different packs, depending on whether they live at the Khmer-style temple of **Phra Phrang Samyod Temple** or the **Sam Phra Karn Shrine**, or whether they dwell on top of the apartment buildings surrounding the downtown. The marauding members of the gangs do get in scrapes, and the losers are taken to the Monkey Hospital, the world's first and only such facility, which is on the grounds of the zoo and open to the public.

Believed to number at least a thousand, the monkeys belong to three closely related species, namely, the crab-eating macaque, the pigtail macaque and the rhesus macaque. They have been living in the city since around the turn of the 17th century when Lopburi was considered the second capital of Siam. Dating from this time, King Narai the Great's Palace is the city's biggest time capsule and within walking distance of the Angkor-era shrines.

Each year, the weirdness factor spikes

in late November when locals put out a gigantic smorgasbord for the monkeys to thank them for bringing so much good fortune, and so many tourist dollars, to the city. The event quickly turns into a feeding frenzy and food fight to rival the most drunken frat party.

Opening Times The Phra Phrang Sam Yot Temple is open from daily from 8 am–6 pm

Address Wichayen Road

Getting There Catch the frequent trains to Lopburi from Bangkok's Hualamphong Station, which take three hours or the buses from Bangkok's Mor Chit Station (two hours) or Ayutthaya (one hour)

Admission Fee 30 baht

18 A Thai Village Homestay
Live, sleep and eat like a local

As the realm of "experiential travel" grows and melds with voluntourism and community-based tourism, visitors crave more and more experiences that blur the boundary lines between cultures and the distinctions between tourists and locals.

To really see the country and the cultures through local eyes, homestays are the best bet. These involve staying with a host family in their home, eating at least two meals a day with them and even visiting the local market or taking a stab at planting rice or going out on a hunt for red ant eggs, sometimes served with omelets and considered a delicacy in the northeast.

Homestays are available all over the country, from the coffee-growing hill-tribes of the mountainous north to the rice-farming lowlanders of the central plains. In this immense field, one small-scale tour operator, stands out. Andaman Discoveries has bagged a series of big awards from companies like Virgin for its dedication to sustainable, ecologically correct and culturally sensitive travel. In 2010, they won the Best Tour Operator, in the category of Responsible Tourism Award, from Wild Asia.

One of their pilot projects took off in **Bahn Talae Nok** ("Village by the Sea") not long after the tsunami killed off a quarter of the 200 villagers. To help the survivors get their heads above water, Andaman Discoveries' founder Bodhi Garrett introduced tourism and home-stays to the village. Visitors can go out fishing with the men, take lessons in batik making, soap making, nipa palm weaving and spicy southern cuisine from the women, or volunteer to teach children in the local school. A mangrove boat trip, kayaking and a visit to a jellyfish farm are other options. The village houses are simple and comfortable and offer a private sleeping area with mattress, pillow, mosquito net and fan. A rotational system managed by the village ensures everyone gets their turn at being a host.

Far from the mainstream media's stereotypes of hostile, Islamic warriors, the Thai Muslims in this area are a peaceable and welcoming people. No alcohol or bikinis are permitted in the village, and this is the whole point of a homestay: to live like a local not a tourist.

Contact Andaman Discoveries, 120/2 Sukapiban 3 Road, Moo 1, Kura, Kuraburi District, Phang Nga Province; +66 (0) 87 917 7165

19 Ko Samui's Wellness Retreats
Healing holidays from yoga to colonics detox

In Southeast Asia, Thailand is the fountainhead of spas and medical tourism. From sheer sensuality to serious surgery, from week-long fasting and colonics irrigation programs to one-hour massages, the range of treatments is as immense as the facilities on offer.

In a vein of travel clotted with competition, the majority of five-star hotels in Thailand now have their own spas. Health resorts devoted to healing, yoga, organic food and New Age treatments are also on the rise.

Ko Samui has a healthy selection of such facilities, such as the country's first so-called "destination health resort", the **Spa Resort** (founded in 1992), the Moroccan-accented **Absolute Sanctuary** and the most lavish and splendidly isolated of them all, the **Kamalaya Wellness Sanctuary**.

Hugging the southeast coastline, the Kamalaya was built around a cave once used by Buddhist monks as a meditation retreat. All these years later, it's still a study in serenity and seclusion. With beachfront villas and hillside bungalows, the resort promises some fantastic views of the sea and surroundings islands.

The natural and spiritual setting makes these programs to counter the stresses of contemporary lifestyles and prevent burnout, or to lose weight, or fast and detox, or get acupuncture and massages, all the healthier. An excellent menu of organic fare and the service is in a league of its own.

The staff at Kamalaya is made up of Western doctors, naturopaths, yoga teachers and practitioners of Chinese traditional medicine. The aim is to provide a harmonious blend of Western and Far Eastern treatments that facilitates a holistic approach to healing that is both physical and emotional. Feel free to make up your own menu of treatments, in consultation with one of the professionals on staff, for whatever ails or strains you.

Having won loads of online plaudits and "destination spa" awards, Kamalaya's mystical allure is grounded in an earthy reality.

Address Kamalaya Ko Samui, 102/9 Moo 3, Laem Set Road, Na-Muang, Ko Samui, Suratthani; +66 (0)7 742 9800; www.kamalaya.com

Getting There Fly to Ko Samui Airport from Bangkok or take one of the ferries operating from the mainland

20 Dining at Soi 38, Sukhumvit
Sublime street eats for a pittance

One of the world's greatest cuisines and arguably the country's most popular export, Thai fare needs to be savored in a genuinely Thai setting: out on the street or alongside a waterway. Pick a stall, pick any food stall on or around Bangkok's legendary **Soi 38** off Sukhumvit, and let the feasting begin, with a staggering variety of high-quality dishes at street-level prices.

Clustered around the north side of the Thonglor Skytrain station straddling Sukhumvit Road are a few stalls for rice noodles and Hainanese-style chicken: boiled or barbecued chicken breasts served on rice with a bowl of broth and a sauce spiced with red and green chili.

The prices are higher here—sometimes around 10 to 20 baht per dish—but the quality is superior to many street stalls around the country and the level of hygiene is impeccable too.

Across the street, Soi 38 is flanked with a hodgepodge of stalls and hole-in-the-wall restaurants. Some of the specialities are braised pork leg, Indonesian-style *satay* sold by the skewer with peanut sauce, Thai-style noodles, oyster omelets, egg noodles served with wontons and red pork, as well as fruit shakes.

The restaurants are nothing fancy. A few soft drink ads, posters of motorcycles and Chinese naturescapes, a Buddhist shrine and portraits of Their Majesties the King and Queen often suffice for décor. The floors are naked concrete, the stools plastic, and for entertainment there may be a TV playing local soap operas. But the lack of ambience is precisely what enhances the food. In fact, it's all about the food. Oftentimes, the dishes here, even though they're mostly basic, are on a par with—or better than—some of the restaurants in five-star hotels, and cost about one-fifth the price.

The vibe is very chilled too. There's no posing or any of the gourmet pretentiousness that makes some upscale restaurants with their upmarket clientele seem so snooty. Most of the restaurants and stalls on Soi 38 have an open-door policy, so you can order from other places and enjoy that all important staple of Thai-defining dining: a familial and communal experience.

Opening Times Most restaurants are open from around 6 pm to midnight

Getting There The Thonglor BTS station is a short stroll to Soi 38 off Sukhumvit

21 Sunset at Promthep Cape

Over the rainbow sunsets at this spectacular location

Prisoners of the urban gulags known more euphemistically as "cities", where smog blacks out the stars and sunsets look like chunks of dirty pink fiberglass insulation, have a deep-seated need to reconnect with nature. That accounts for much of the tropics' appeal and romantic nature.

Taking in a multihued sunset from **Promthep Cape**, the rocky headland that juts out into the sea at the southwest of Phuket, is practically a rite of passage on the island. It's demographics cheating popularity means it's also big with lovers, families and gaggles of friends. Come dusk, the island's southernmost extremity becomes an enormous viewing platform as the sun goes down in a blaze of red, purple and magenta glory. Not surprisingly, the cape is the island's most photographed location.

Named after Brahma, the Supreme Being in the Hindu trinity, Promthep Cape certainly looks like an enchanted realm during the twilight hour. The cape's often-visited shrine to the deity imparts even more mythical importance to the scene. Surrounding the four-faced image enshrined in marble are hundreds of wooden elephants, for Brahma's heavenly steed is a tusker with 33 heads.

A lighthouse, some 60 meters above sea level, which also doubles as a museum and houses interesting maritime artifacts, sheds some light on both the history and the geography of this area, which is rich in seafarer's lore. The lighthouse was built in homage to the 50th anniversary of King Rama's Accession to the throne in 1996.

For many drivers on a daytrip circling the island's beaches, the viewpoint is the penultimate, pre-dinner stop: a prelude and all-natural pyrotechnics show before heading for supper at one of the island's many superb seafood restaurants.

Partly spiritual, partly natural, partly regal and completely unmissable, sunset-gazing from Promthep Cape is such a blazingly powerful experience that you won't even need digital images to keep that scene seared into your memory banks.

Address Rawai Beach, Phuket

Getting There Hire a car or motorbike or go as part of a tour group

CHAPTER 2
EXPLORING THAILAND

Thailand offers a rich and varied experience for the traveler who takes the time to get to know the place. From Bangkok, with its royal temples, immense shopping centres and numerous museums, to the ancient capital of Ayutthaya, and from the seaside playgrounds of Pattaya, Phuket and Ko Samui to the cultural heartland of Chiang Mai and the Golden Triangle, there is plenty to delight everyone.

Exploring Bangkok
Rattanakosin District; Dusit District; Khaosan Road; Chinatown & Little India

Exploring Central Thailand
Khao Yai National Park; Kanchanaburi; Ayutthaya; Lopburi; Hua Hin; Pattaya; Onward Journeys

Exploring Chiangmai & the North
The Old City; Day 2; Night 2

Exploring Phuket
Day 1; Day 2

Exploring Ko Samui
Chaweng; Bang Rak; Bo Phut; Mae Nam; Snake Farm & Waterfalls; Mummified Monk; Bound for Lamai; After Dark Carousing

Exploring Southern Thailand
Khao Lak; Khao Sok National Park; Ko Ra; Ko Phra Thong; Ko Maphrao; Ko Yao Noi; Trang; Ko Lipe; Andaman Discoveries

Exploring the Great Northeast
Nakhon Ratchasima; Phimai Historical Park; Land of the Dinosaurs; Buri Ram; Surin; Mekong Odysseys; Nong Khai; Chiang Khan; Loei

Top: Temple in Chiang Mai.
Center: Bridge over the River Kwai.
Below far left: Long-necked hilltribe woman living in Northern Thailand.
Below center left: Chumpon Reef, Ko Tao.
Below right: The Verandah, Mandarin Oriental, Bangkok.

**EXPLORING
BANGKOK**
A journey into Bangkok's
glorious past and present

Wat Saket

From a backwater in the 17th century that was little more than a port of call for boats sailing to the former royal capital of Ayutthaya, the tiny hamlet once known as Bang Makok ("Village of Olive Plums") has morphed into a juggernaut of 10 million.

In 1782, it became the new capital and citadel, encircled by natural moats, of the still-reigning Chakri dynasty of kings. The cornerstone of the new kingdom was the Grand Palace, which remains the city's most visited attraction.

Long before the palace was constructed, however, it was a Thai tradition since the first empire of Sukhothai (circa the 13th century AD) to build a temple on the grounds of the palace. So, in front of the Grand Palace is the illustrious Temple of the Emerald Buddha, showing off the country's most venerable image. In this way, Bangkok has preserved the capital gains and ancient customs of preceding kingdoms.

National Museum

Rattanakosin District
Bangkok's venerable historic center

The city's most historic part is justly renowned for having tons of "must see" temples, but their styles and extras lend them different auras. **Wat Pho** has a massage center as well as a nearby school for hands-on classes in this ancient healing art, while **Loha Prasat** (the "Metal Temple") has 37 spires made out of metal that symbolize the spiky road to enlightenment. Across the street from it is **Wat Saket**, crowned by the Golden Mount, enshrining a relic of the Buddha from Nepal.

The area's biggest improvement in recent years is the addition of two more high-tech museums that have rendered the dowdy and dusty **National Museum** almost obsolete. Both the **Rattanakosin Exhibition Hall** and the **Museum of Siam** feature multimedia exhibitions and interactive displays that bring history to virtual life in thought-evoking ways.

The **Tah Chang Pier** in Rattankosin is a launching pad for exploring the canals of Thonburi, the **Royal Barges Museum**, and further down the river, **Wat Arun** or the Temple of Dawn. The riverside temple is a testament to how Siam, rather than yielding to the influence of colonial powers, assimilated them.

The blueprint for the five towers of this riverfront temple bears the stamp of Khmer master builders, but the broken crockery, in florid patterns, is Chinese, and the gods enshrined in the niches of the tower are Hindu. Yet the end result still seems distinctly Thai and much more than the sum of its disparate parts.

Dusit District
Boasting a regal lineage

The district of Dusit, enclosing both the **Royal Family's Chitralada Palace** and the British-looking **Parliament Buildings**, has a regal lineage. King Rama V's former palace of **Wimanmek**, which is the world's biggest golden teakwood mansion, is the zenith of **Dusit Park**. Still one of the best days out in Bangkok, the park is home to other museums devoted to photographs taken by the present king, sacred white elephant lore, royal carriages, clocks and

the handiwork of rural artisans in the **Abhisek Dusit Throne Hall**. With its flourishes, arabesques and exquisite fretwork lifted from Moorish architecture, the hall is a work of architectural art.

Wimanmek was actually constructed on the island of Ko Si Chang, near Pattaya, in 1868 and used as a summer palace for royalty. In 1901, it was dismantled piece by piece and moved to its present location. The reconstruction took 19 months. Not a single nail was used to put it together. Instead, the builders used wooden pegs.

The 31 rooms open to the public are splendidly decorated with blue and white Chinese porcelains, sepia photos, golden cutlery forged in England, chairs upholstered with crocodile skins and the largest topaz gemstone in the world.

You can also sneak a peek at King Rama V's private quarters and bathroom, which has the first shower in Thailand, a chair for a commode, and a crystal chamber pot. There are free tours of the mansion, in English and Thai, beginning

Abhisek Dusit Throne Hall

at 9.35 am. The compulsory tours, approximately 30–40 minutes long, depart every 15 minutes. The last one leaves at 3.15 pm.

Within walking distance is **Dusit Zoo**. Once used by Rama V as his private botanical garden, the zoo now covers a total of 14 hectares, two-thirds of which is land, with around 288 different species of mammals, more than 1,000 kinds of birds and almost 300 species of reptiles. The pedal boats on the man-made lake and the **Happy Land Amusement Park** ensure that this is a prime spot for picnicking and big days out with the family in tow.

Khaosan Road
Center of the backpacker's universe

Southeast Asia's most famous strip for backpackers is still abuzz with energy almost 30 years since the guesthouses began sprouting up. The best reason to come is the informal street party every night when travelers from all over the map mingle with trendy Thais, street vendors and masseuses galore.

During the day, or the purple dusk, hit the **Santichai Prakan Park** on Phra Arthit near the pier on the river. The whitewashed fort, where swallows nest in the mouths of cannons, is a backdrop for jugglers, dancers, aerobics exercisers and sporadic music and theater festivals. The Thai restaurants on this strip, like the long-running Hemlock, serve up authentic fare in cosmopolitan settings.

Chinatown & Little India
Slices of life served raw

These clamorous and chaotic districts are an urban planner's wildest nightmare, but for visitors who relish a little bit of grit to balance out all the mall-heavy glitz, they are pulsating with life and offer deep insights into two of the kingdom's cornerstones of culture.

Most of **Chinatown**'s draws are located on or around the two main drags of

Khaosan Road

Old Market, Chinatown

Yaowarat and Charoen Krung. They run parallel to each other, eventually merging at the Chinese-style arch near **Wat Traimit**, home of a solid gold Buddha. According to the principles of *feng shui*, the sinuous Yaowarat resembles a dragon. So it's auspicious for business.

For a whirlwind tour of Chinatown, several stopovers are essential. First is **Wat Neng Noi Yee** (sometimes known as Wat Mangkon Kamalwat), the kingdom's most important center of Mahayana Buddhism, with elements of Confucianism and Taoism. Outside the front gates, on Charoen Krung Road, are shops selling cardboard TVs, cars, mobile phones and paper money used as burnt offerings for ancestors and friends to use in the afterlife.

Off Yaowarat, down a little lane called Trok Itsaranuphap, is a Chinese archway that leads into the two-century-ancient **Old Market**. The vendors sit on top of big stone platforms inside the market hawking an array of fresh fish, ducks and chickens. It's worth a little trip through here just to see such slices of daily life served raw.

Little India, or Pahurat, is smaller but no less rambunctious. Across the country, Indian tailors have the market all sewn up. That's why the area's main attraction remains the **Pahurat Market**, alongside the street of the same name. Although the market is known for its incredible selection of fabrics—cotton, Thai silk and batik—the two floors of stalls inside also have saris, gaudy paintings of Hindu deities, Indian CDs and Bollywood DVDs.

Close to here, the **Sri Guru Singh Sabha Temple** is the second largest Sikh temple outside of India. To show you how the area is slowly changing, next to it stands the **India Emporium**. Over four air-conditioned floors, the mall is adding more threads of popular and classical Indian culture to the area's tapestry of multiple ethnicities.

Shopping Sprees

For serial shoppers, Bangkok is a gigantic bazaar. The city's extremities are revealed in what are your two main choices: malls and street markets. Ideally, any shopping safari should

Siam Paragon

include a combination of both; the street markets are full of local color and bargains, whereas the air-conditioned malls are retreats from the sweltering heat, with Cineplexes and food courts.

Another big difference is that you have to haggle over prices at the markets, but the malls have fixed prices. When bartering, it's a general rule of thumb to ask the price from the vendor, then offer them about 40-50 percent of that and try to meet in the middle.

Most of the malls are located in urban—and urbane—areas like **Siam Square**, which encapsulates **MBK**, the **Siam Discovery Center** and the upper end **Siam Paragon** that contains an Imax Cinema and the aquarium **Siam Ocean World**. Within walking distance is **CentralWorld** (the risen phoenix that was razed to the rafters during the protests of 2010), and the super chic **Gaysorn Plaza**, resplendent with big brand names like Prada, Christian Dior and Burberry.

The Emporium (BTS Phrom Pong) is the biggest and priciest catwalk on Sukhumvit Road, which is also where the community mall trend has been set in concrete with K Village, Playground and the "thriller boutique mall" Mansion 7 with its façade of a haunted house.

Panthip Plaza and **Fortune Town** are hard-wired for IT buffs and gamers. For weekend shopping sprees head to **Chatuchak Market** (see page 15).

Eating Out

The Thai penchant for eating and snacking means Bangkok is a movable feast 24/7. Few cities offer as many international flavors priced on such a sliding scale that climbs from holes-in-the-wall and food stalls to the stratosphere of 60-stories-steep rooftop opulence and haute cuisine.

For upscale Thai fare, **Bo.lan** is the order of the day. Choose from quintessential favorites like the "Southern-style orange curry with fish" or the "Balance Menu" that mixes and matches the main Thai flavors. The beautifully appointed restaurant on Sukhumvit Soi 26 is also the home of the **Slow Food Bangkok Chapter** where they hold regular workshops and tasting sessions.

As one of the city's main stomachs, Sukhumvit is where you'll find classic Italian dishes at **La Bella Napoli**, the roadhouse-flavored **Fat Gutz Saloon**, archetypal pub grub at the **Bull's Head** and the **Dubliner** and, for comic relief and novelty value, the **Flying Chicken Restaurant** where waiters on unicycles catch cooked chickens on skewers attached to a motorcycle helmet.

Face is another staple of the area, with Thai, Japanese and Indian fare served in the authentic ambience of a traditional Thai wooden house.

The big hotels are enclaves of fine dining, with **Lord Jim's**, a seafood spe-cialist in the Mandarin Oriental hotel, and **Nahm** in the Metropolitan standing out amongst the strong competition. The latter is the creation of chef David Thompson, awarded the first Michelin star for a Thai restaurant in London.

Carousing After Dark

Once known more for its titillation factor than its sophistication, Bangkok's night-life has become a cosmopolitan act.

Nightspots like **Q Bar** now bring in big-name DJs; **Khaosan Road** is a veritable Mardi Gras of backpacking revelers every night; **RCA** is a hotbed of dance clubs for Thai youth; **Silom Soi 4** plays to a predominantly gay crowd; and a bevy of English and Irish pubs provide comfort zones for visitors and expats with a hankering for home.

In recent years, new enclaves of chic nightspots have cropped up around Sukhumvit Soi 55 and Soi 63, such as **Iron Fairies** (an industrial-style jazz, cocktails and gourmet burgers venue), a spin-off club called **Clouds** that looks like a transplanted chunk of New York's Soho, and the more Bohemian **WTF Cafe and Gallery**.

Bedding Down

The oversupply of rooms in Bangkok is a boon for visitors. Even the new five stars like the **St. Regis** (every guest has their own butler), the **Hansar** (which quickly shot to number one on Trip Advisor) and the river-view standbys (the **Mandarin Oriental**, the **Shangri-la** and the **Peninsula**) are cheap in comparison to much of the Southeast Asian competition.

In the burgeoning boutique genre, Bangkok also fares well. Properties like the **Arun Residence** and the **Old Bangkok Inn** impress with their dedica-tion to recreating the arts and charms of yesteryear's Siam.

The repercussions of another building boom are being felt across the mid-range sector as budget-conscious travelers opt for two- and three-star accommodations like **ibis** and the Dutch-owned **Golden Tulip** chain.

Long-stay visitors can go for serviced apartments, while the backpacker brigade is well catered for in the glut of guesthouses around Khaosan Road.

Mandarin Oriental

EXPLORING CENTRAL THAILAND
From ancient temple ruins to guided jungle treks

Within a few hours' drive from Bangkok is the country's oldest and largest national park, Khao Yai, and a small city, Lopburi, overrun by monkeys, whereas the neon Babylon of Pattaya contrasts sharply with Ayutthaya, renowned for its UNESCO-designated "Ancient City", while the sea vista resorts of Hua Hin and Pranburi draw an older crowd and a throng of upwardly mobile locals.

Khao Yai National Park
Astonishing natural diversity

The preferred daytrip for urbanites fleeing Bangkok on weekends, the park's natural grandeur and its cornucopia of creatures has not been diminished by all the people, who are still mere specks in this 2,168 square kilometer epic tableaux of mountainous verdure.

To really explore "Big Mountain" you'll need to stay over for a night at one of the many resorts in the nearby town of **Pak Chong**. Almost all of them arrange tours. On the lower end of the price scale, there's Greenleaf Guesthouse & Tour (the owner has acquired the nickname "Birdman" for his bird watching tours), while at the higher end is the extravagant Muthi Maya Forest Pool Village resort.

Some visitors may shun the guides and organized treks over the 50 kilometers of hiking trails, but those Indiana Jones imitators and solo adventurers could easily miss a pit viper sleeping on a branch, the claw marks left on a tree trunk by a Malaysian sunbear in search of bee hives, the secret spots favored by guar (a rare species of wild cattle) or the trampled grass indicating wild elephants are near that only the professional guides can spot.

The park is open all year round. During the soggy season, however, leeches are common. Other options near the park are tours and wine tasting sessions at **Khao Yai Winery** and **GranMonte** or a visit to the area's **"Little Tuscany"**.

Rainforest in Khao Yai National Park

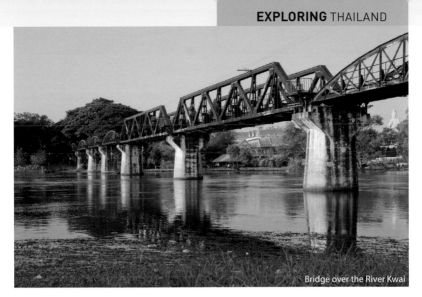
Bridge over the River Kwai

Kanchanaburi
Infamous World War II historic site

This province is synonymous with World War II. From countless calamities and numerous casualties inflicted when Allied and Asian POWs were forced by their Japanese captors to build the infamous "Death Railway", a number of epitaphs and landmarks have arisen, most notably the **Bridge Over the River Kwai**; the **Kanchanaburi War Cemetery** in the eponymous capital; and 90 minutes from town, the **Hellfire Pass Memorial**, which is a museum and walking trail. Many of the tours offered by local resorts include stopovers at all these sites in addition to more adventurous options like bamboo rafting and elephant riding.

Every year, in December, a festival serves as a series of remembrance days for those who fought against fascism.

Kanchanaburi is also a haven for "floating rafthouse hotels" on the strip, with the backpacker favorite the **Jolly Frog** and river-straddling properties like the five-star **Felix Resort**, which has brilliant views of the infamous bridge.

Out and around the mainstay for eco-excursions, **Erawan National Park**, is the beautifully appointed **River Kwai Resotel** and another clutch of resorts not far from the **Sai Yoke Waterfall**.

Kanchanaburi's most contentious attraction is the Tiger Temple. Enough reports have surfaced from NGOs insisting that it's a glorified tourist trap guilty of mistreating the tigers kept there for photo ops with visitors, to make the operation seem more than a mite suspicious.

Ayutthaya
Thailand's most glorious ruins

From Bangkok all you'll have to spend to reach the ancient capital by train is about 90 minutes and one US dollar.

Outside of Angkor Wat and Sukhothai in central Thailand, the city's 400 crumbling temples and myriad Buddha images decapitated or dismembered by invaders from Burma, constitute the most glorious ruins in Southeast Asia. Located in the city's spleen, the **Historical Park** is best traversed by bicycle (for the fit) or *tuk-tuk* (for the slack). To rent a bicycle,

Elephant ride tour at Ayutthaya

(a mixture of Thai and Chinese styles) and **Wat Phutthaisawan** (complete with a large reclining Buddha image meant to symbolize his passage into nirvana).

After doing a round trip of the island by boat in the late afternoon, the pier is near the night bazaar, where a jumble of food stalls with English menus serve up classic Thai dishes in an alfresco setting overlooking a waterway tattooed with multihued fluorescent lights at night.

go to the shops on Soi 1, where you will also find an array of inexpensive accommodations and decent restaurants.

Surrounded by a natural "moat" of three rivers, the city is crisscrossed with canals and circumnavigated by long-tail boats. You can charter them from the pier near the **Chandra Kasem Palace**, which is also a museum. The boats include stops at the more stupendous riverside temples, such as **Wat Phanan Choeng**

Many daytrippers combine an excursion to Ayutthaya with a stopover at the **Bang Pa In Summer Palace**, before heading back to Bangkok. If staying over for a night in order to explore the more far-flung ruins, the **Baan Thai House** has beautiful wooden bungalows, a spa, pool and nicely landscaped gardens, far enough from the city center to be a safe house from urban worries.

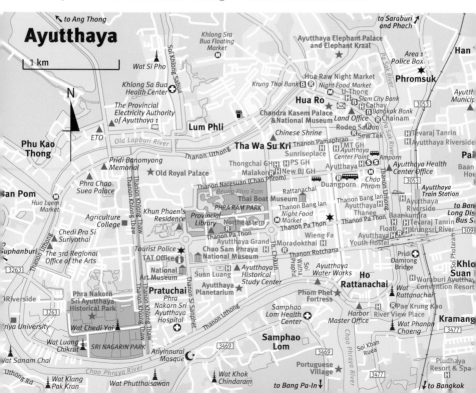

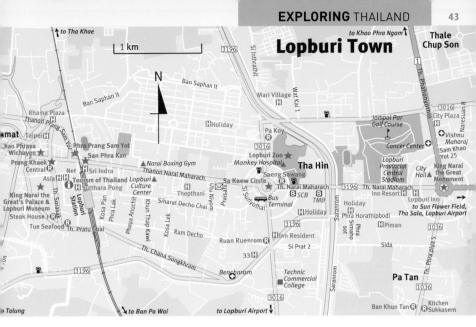

Lopburi
Monkeys rule the town

Once considered Siam's second capital back in the 17th century, this small city on the central plains is celebrated for its regal connections and a horde of macaques living in the downtown core around the centuries-old Khmer-looking **Phra Phrang Samyod Temple** or the shrine of **Sam Phra Karn**.

Numbering around a thousand, the monkeys' high-wire antics on the streets attract a steady stream of visitors, highly bemused until the miscreants try to steal their cameras and sunglasses.

Monkey watching may be the city's Darwinian pull, but situated near there is **King Narai the Great's Palace**. Also on the grounds is the **Lopburi Museum** which dusts off the past to make the area's history shine.

The city's hotels, mostly within walking distance of the palatial museum, are on the spartan side. For more luxury, check out and in to the **Lopburi Inn Hotel**.

If staying over for a night, the zoo with its **Monkey Hospital** is an entertaining itinerary filler. Onward journeys, either to Ayutthaya, back to Bangkok or up to Chiang Mai, are easy, thanks to a well-connected network of buses and trains.

The city's big day out, however, comes every November when local authorities organize a vegetarian feast for the macaques (seen as minions of the Hindu monkey god Hanuman) that turns into a melee of slapstick proportions with loads of snap-happy visitors on hand to frame the action.

Hua Hin
Historic beach resort

Hua Hin's nickname, the "Queen of Tranquility", has been challenged by a number of residential and tourist-minded developments in recent years. Other than Pattaya, the closest beach resort to Bangkok is undergoing a building boom, with new hotels and condos going up. That doesn't mean its chief strengths have been weakened though.

Wongamart Beach, Pattaya

Hua Hin is still a clubhouse for golfers with the **Springfield Royal** and the **Royal Hua Hin** (built in 1927) perennially popular and extremely affordable. In fact, King Rama VII was in the middle of a golf game here when informed that his government had been overthrown, paving the way for Thailand to become a constitutional monarchy back in 1932.

Traces of Hua Hin's legacy as the kingdom's first beach resort and royalty's favorite retreat are not lost but still found in the railway station that's a work of wooden art, resplendent with fantastic fretwork. Apart from the extravagant hotel chains, such as the Marriott, Hilton, Hyatt and Anantara, Hua Hin's most historic lodgings are in the **Sofitel**. This vision of pan-colonial splendor dates back to 1923. In the mid-1980s, it served as the French Embassy in the Oscar-winning film *The Killing Fields*.

One of Hua Hin's principal pleasures is its many seafood restaurants enhanced with oceanic vistas. All the major hotels have F&B outlets where gluttony dines with gastronomy, but they are pricey. In the middle of the city, the **Chatchai Market** whips up great Thai dishes for a pittance amidst a boisterous atmosphere.

Moving on? In the city's waiting room is **Chiva Som**, the exorbitant wellness center with a celebrity-heavy list of clients. And situated some 60 kilometers south is **Khao Sam Roi Yot National Park**, replete with photogenic beaches, limestone hills and spooky caves.

Pattaya
The extremities of nightlife and daylight

Few cities in Southeast Asia excite such an extreme reaction from both visitors and expats. For some this is the modern-day equivalent of Sodom and Gomorrah: a town steeped in sex, sin and liquor. But if you stay away from all the go-go bars on **Walking Street** and the beer bars on and off **Beach Road**, Pattaya becomes a more family-friendly destination.

That's particularly true over on the Jomtien Beach side. An influx of high-end properties like the Hilton has given the city a more cosmopolitan makeover. To really lose the urban vibe, head for the all-in-one hotels of Jomtien.

Pattaya's trump card is its diversity of activities. This is the perfect place for both hyperactive kids and terminally youthful fathers with energy and calories to burn. Take your pick from paintball, go-karts, golf, horseback riding, sailing, windsurfing, scuba diving, and a hodge-podge of theme parks.

Pattaya's other selling point is how economical it is. Price-gouging competition in the hotel and bar sectors is an equation that equals some substantial savings.

Onward Journeys
Quieter climes and boutique resorts

Many Thais, along with a smattering of expats and vacationers, prefer the quieter climes of **Cha Am**, while **Pranburi** (25 km from Hua Hin) is also shedding some of its sleepy reputation with a bunch of boutique resorts like the **Ali Baba** and five-star developments like the Moroccan-style **Villa Maroc**.

EXPLORING
CHIANGMAI & THE NORTH
Nature, outdoor activities,
crafts and hilltribe culture

I n 2011, when the Thai government put a promotional drive into fourth gear to have a city nominated for UNESCO's list of the world's most artistic and design-savvy cities, Chiang Mai was the country's first and most natural choice to compete in the category of "Crafts and Folk Art".

Long a nucleus of new-wave crafts and age-old antiquities, the "Northern Rose" has been experiencing a renaissance as the country's young visionaries tire of Bangkok and relocate here. Combine these enticements with mountain views, a hospitable climate and a whole lot of highland detours brimming with hill-tribe exotica, and it's clear that Thailand's second city is really first rate.

Another substantial attribute is that the people are welcoming and charmingly soft-spoken, the northern dialect a lullaby for the ears.

The Old City
Old culture and magical charm

S urrounded by weatherworn walls and ancient gates, the city's aorta pulsates with the rhythms of travelers passing through and the echoes of history.

Set aside a day to explore its intricacies. Hit the temples first for an eyeful of northern art and soul. **Wat Phra Singh**, with its low sweeping roofs, is a paragon of northern architecture. The temple is also a trophy case that contains the city's most revered Buddha image.

Also not to miss is **Wat Chedi Luang**, a relic from the 15th century that once contained the Emerald Buddha now housed in Bangkok, and still encompasses the city pillar, a spiritual power plug for animism's true believers.

For other derivations on a Buddhist theme, try **Wat Chiang Man**. Dating to the 13th century, the main pillar of the community is buttressed with sacred white elephants.

Wat Phra Singh

Lunch Time
Temple slogging under a broiling sun is thirsty work. Among the restaurants of the old city, visitors are never starved for choice. When in Chiang Mai, why not try a northern specialty from an authentically local eatery? **Kow Soy Siri Soy** on Inthawarorot Road serves up the northern-style noodles known as *khao soy* for a pittance in unpretentious surroundings.

Historic Vista
In the afternoon, drop by the old city's **Chiang Mai City Arts & Cultural Center** for some background on local

history and hilltribes, or the **Chiang Mai Women's Prison Massage Center** where you can get a massage and become a philanthropist simultaneously (the program gives the inmates a certifiable skill).

Afterwards, make tracks for the city's most towering landmark, **Doi Suthep**. This mountaintop temple stands some 1,066 meters above sea level, commanding Napoleonic views of the city and countryside. Trams run from the parking lot all the way up to the main temple, where Buddhist and Hindu elements converge in a montage of sacred snakes, monkeys and tuskers juxtaposed against Buddha images, strolling monks and, to top it off, a copper-plated *chedi* burnished with sunlight.

Night Bazaar & Shopping

In the city's deck of after-dark distractions, this is one of the biggest drawing cards. And it's a wild card too, sprawling in, on and around **Chang Klan Road**. The market is so large it takes hours to scope it out.

Some of the stalls open in the late afternoon, but it's not business and bedlam as usual until 8 pm or so, when the highly contagious shopping virus reaches a fever pitch. On sale is a glut of products running the gamut from handicrafts and Thai kitsch to knock-off sneakers, polo shirts, DVDs, wooden carvings and hilltribe regalia. Many of the goods are not endemic to Chiang Mai. They are on offer at **Chatuchak Market** and at the night markets around Patpong and Sukhumvit Roads in Bangkok too.

Of the bespoke services, portrait painters are quite possibly the most popular.

The bazaar is also a great place to eat, drink and be harried. (Admittedly, some of the hard-sell touts and wandering

Chiang Mai night street market

Akha frog vendors can be as pesky and annoying as flies, but that's the tax you pay for this stampede of unbridled capitalism.)

For a respite from the rustling, or to relish some inexpensive Thai dishes, head for the **Anusarn Market**. Among the old eateries, **Ping Ping Seafood and Thai Food** scores high marks. Alternatively, head for the refueling stations of food stalls and the free shows of Thai dance and music in the **Galare Food Court.**

Another welcome service in the **Night Bazaar** is open-air massage chairs sure to refresh you for another round of conspicuous consumption followed by chill-out drinks at the bars and pubs clustered around the crossroads of **Loi Kroh** and **Chang Klan**.

For other shopping alternatives, the **Saturday Walking Street** on Wua Lai Road (south of the old city) and the **Sunday Walking Street** on Ratchadamnoen Road (in the old town) are more than just excuses to shop until your bank balance drops a few zeros. Both are excellent afternoons and nights out abuzz with arts and entertainment.

Since many of the vendors are the same, the selection of clothes, handicrafts and Lanna-style keepsakes is not all that different.

Bedding Down

The city's funkiest new digs, the **Dusit D2 Chiang Mai**, is smack dab in the middle of the Night Bazaar. The hotel's *Wallpaper*-worthy design and super-cool F&B outlets, **Moxie and Mix Bar**, appeal to a younger, hipper set.

Another cornerstone of convenience, but situated in the old city, is **U Chiang Mai Hotel**. This boutique hotel has an incredible range of bespoke services, a 24-hour gym, free yoga classes a couple of times a week, amenities like iPod docking stations and maybe the best breakfasts in town. It's a family-chummy hotel too.

Also in this neck of the historic woods is the backpacker ghetto of **Moon Muang Soi 7 and 9**. Considering all the competition and price gouging in the hotel sector, you shouldn't need to go this far down market.

Chiang Mai's upper end is defined by the sprawling **Mandarin Oriental Hotel Dara Dhevi**. Spread over 24 hectares,

this is a resort unto itself. The design flourishes, artfully melding Lanna, Burmese, Chinese and colonial touches, are astounding. Now imagine looking out your window and seeing that your villa is in the middle of a rice paddy with guests traversing the grounds in horse-drawn carriages.

Farther out of town but no less opulent is the **Four Seasons Resort Chiang Mai**, surrounded by mountains and rice terraces. The 64 pavilions and a dozen pool villas are handsomely decked out in teak and embellished with Thai-style verandahs. For the penultimate paramours' heart-to-heart, try the exclusive and alfresco dinner for two under a candelabra of moon and stars at the **Rice Barn**.

Day 2

Chiang Mai has enough top-notch attractions to keep most visitors tied up for a week. So those on shorter sojourns will have to choose wisely.

Consistently ranked number one among the city's activities on TripAdvisor, a phenomenal full day out at the **Patara Elephant Camp** requires learning how to ride, command and bathe a beast held

Patara Elephant Camp

sacred by many Thais. Not just the largest living land animal, but the only creature besides humans that mourn their dead, the perilously endangered elephant casts a suitably huge spell over both adults and children; truly an only-in-Thailand experience.

Sure to be another pinnacle of anyone's trip, the **Flight of the Gibbon** is a zipline adventure replete with rainforest backdrops and heart-pounding action. The company also offers a number of options, including homestays and waterfall odysseys.

For gourmands or gluttons in search of the slow lane, cooking schools have mushroomed across the city, but for something a tad more exotic try the **Thai Farm Cooking School**. It's located on an organic farm outside the city where prospective Thai chefs can get hands-on experience in concocting their very own sweet green curry and also see the gardens where all those herbs are grown.

Another enclave of local dishes and ingredients is the **Warorot Market**. In 2011, it was duly feted with exhibitions and tributes for its centenary. As the centerpiece of the Kad Luang community, near the Ping River, the three-story

market is the largest such venue in the north. To see slices of daily life served raw, and an array of goods, the market is an essential stop on any itinerary. After dark, it turns into a night market spilling onto the streets.

As a microcosm of tolerant, polyglot Thailand, this community is exemplary. During a short walk you can see the city's oldest Chinese shrine (**Chao Por Pung Tao Kong**), a Hindu temple, a mosque, a Namdharis temple (they are offshoots of the Sikh faith) and many Buddhist places of worship.

Night 2

Doing some feasting and carousing alongside the Ping River is a pleasure to be savored. Some of the better choices are **Le Coq d'Or Restaurant**, in business for more than 25 years now (which is about five centuries in the restaurant trade) and the **River Ping Palace**, a sumptuous collection of teak houses owned by French expats.

For a few drinks with a chaser of live rock 'n' blues, check out the **Riverside** and its next-door neighbor the **Brasserie**.

Over in the old part of town, the **Writer's Club and Wine Bar** caters to an older clientele, heavy on expats, in search of good conversation, not deafening music. The **Northgate Jazz Bar**, just inside the Chang Phuak Gate to the north, stars local and visiting musicians in an intimate venue. Also in this neighborhood is the new location of the **Darling Wine Pub**, the city's oldest wine bar, which is famously gay-friendly.

Spicy, on Chiang Moi Road, remains the last chance saloon and after-hours pick-up joint. Long after the other nightspots have closed at 1 am, this techno disco is still noisy and a bit sleazy.

Warorot Market

Elephant trekking

Chiang Mai and **Crank Adventures**, provide a variety of excursions fit for all levels, more grueling multi-day packages for experts, or combinations that include biking, rafting and rock climbing.

Onward Journeys

From Chiang Mai, many younger travelers head for the hills of **Pai**, a backpacker town that has a few more upscale offerings and some beautifully atmospheric riverside accommodations.

It's also a departure point for treks, as are the bigger cities in the north, such as **Mae Hong Son** and **Chiang Rai**. The latter is quickly becoming a quieter and more idyllic alternative to Chiang Mai.

For thrill seekers, another popular activity is renting a motorcycle to do a loop from Chiang Mai through the mountains of Mae Hong Son province, which are wreathed with fog in the early mornings and dappled with gigantic sunflowers when the cool season begins to bite in November. **Mae Sariang**, a pastoral hamlet close to the border with Myanmar, makes for a restful pit stop.

Trekking

Chiang Mai is the base camp for treks of the northern highlands. Usually they tend to mix and match a few basic ingredients like elephant rides, bamboo rafting and temple visits with bursts of trekking and stopovers in hilltribe villages for rest and reconnaissance. On the one-day tours, you'll be back in Chiang Mai for sundowner drinks, but on the multi-day treks, you'll sleep over in hilltribe villages, an eye-opening experience replete with basic boot camp amenities. To go upscale, without skimping on the sightseeing or culture, however, try the sumptuous **Lisu Lodge**.

Because there are so many different trekking companies in Chiang Mai, and so many hotels also arrange them, the rates are rock bottom and the quality is standardized.

Treks depart all year round, though the rainy season from May to October can yield more spills than thrills. Beware that in the mountains the mercury can plummet to freezing point in December and January. Definitely put a jacket and sweater in your daypack.

Cycling Hub

Chiang Mai is also the mountain biking hub of Southeast Asia. A number of reliable outfits, like **Mountain Biking**

Mon Jam Hill

EXPLORING PHUKET
Spectacular scenery and warm blue seas on a fun island

Thailand's biggest island and richest province is endowed with sunspots galore, wellness retreats, palatial pool villas and rambunctious nightlife. It also has its share of hidden coves and slices of serenity. In addition to being the premier water sports center in Thailand for everything from diving to sea kayaking and big game fishing, Phuket has a green heart and mountainous spine. Because of its width, girth, and the lengthy A to Z list of activities on offer, it's best to first decide where you want to stay and then arrange your itinerary accordingly.

Day 1

To get the lay of the island, start the morning with a drive down the western coast, beginning at **Mai Khao**. Cheap and plentiful car and jeep rentals are one of Thailand's best bargains, or hire a driver as well for maximum sightseeing pleasure.

Towards the northern end of the island, not far from the international airport, **Mai Khao Bay** sits pretty. This is the bipolar opposite of Phuket's most popular beach, **Patong**. Indeed, it's something of a Robinson Crusoe kind of experience that also makes for a pleasant early morning beach stroll.

A few five-star resorts, such as the **Anantara** and the **JW Marriott**, provide refuges for visitors with deep pockets. More recently, the Marriott chain opened the **Renaissance Resort & Spa**, where sea and sand are reflected in the design. And on the grounds of the **West Sands Resort**, the **Splash Jungle Waterpark**

Patong Beach

Phuket's luxury villas

has been making waves with kids. Another family-friendly favorite is the new **Holiday Inn Mai Khao**, where you should enjoy a gourmet buffet breakfast in J's Café & Restaurant and where kids eat for free.

Also in this part of the island is the legendary **Blue Canyon Country Club** with golf on "The Canyon" or "The Lakes", courses, a spa and fine dining.

For a shopping or coffee break, the uniquely designed **Turtle Village** complex, featuring a Jim Thompson outlet for Thai silk products, is the default setting.

Millionaire's Mile

Keep heading south, as this thread of tarmac in Phuket's tapestry is embellished with oceanic vistas and sunglazed beaches, past the beaches of **Nai Yang**, **Nai Thon** and the scenically deserted **Surin**, to the stretch known as the "**Millionaire's Mile**". Captains of industry sailing the high seas of international finance use these beaches as ports in a storm of stress and strain.

The number of glitzy holiday homes is matched by some of the opulent accommodations, such as the **Villa Andalaya** and **Village Andara**, where the pool villas or homes with up to six bedrooms go for US$1,000–5,000 dollars per night.

Down at the tip of Surin is **Pansea Beach**, an exclusive cove backed by the equally exclusive resorts **Amanpuri Phuket** and **Chedi**, where aristocrats and the glitterati escape from all the tawdry tabloids and muckrakers.

Farther down the coast, have lunch at the legendary **Baan Rim Pa** (definitely reserve a table in advance during the high season) at the north end of Patong Beach. It's perched on the precipice of a cliff, with stunning sea vistas and a soundtrack of waves getting whitewashed by the rocks.

Patong Beach

Phuket's most famous and splashiest beach is awash with high-end hotels, seafood restaurants, street vendors, tons of touts and the priciest *tuk-tuk* drivers in the kingdom ("Hey boss"). It's also the busiest and most Westernized part of the island and thus a comfort zone for lost and disoriented souls.

For a run-down on Phuket's mind-boggling array of activities, from kayaking to cooking classes, golf and ATV tours, pop into some of the travel agents located here. Competition keeps price gouging to a minimum.

In the early afternoon, take a swimming break at **Patong Beach** and rent a deck chair to wait out the mad-dog heat.

For some retail therapy, if sun worshipping is not your thing, visit the state-of-the-art **Patong Promenade** mall.

Kata & Karon

Keep heading south. After Patong, these two beaches seem a world away. Both appeal to older, more family-oriented crowds.

Karon, one of the longest beaches on the island, is particularly popular with package tourists from Scandinavia, which is reflected in some of the pubs and restaurants around here, whereas **Kata** is smaller, younger and renowned for being the country's main surfing spot, with waves high enough during the monsoon season to give surfers wet dreams.

One of Karon's most novel attractions is the **Dino Park Mini Golf** near Karon Beach. In the park, high-tech effects such as an active volcano promise a hole-in-one of sheer fun.

Both of these beaches offer a splendid selection of hotels and restaurants. Just off Kata is the legend-spawning **Boathouse**. Renovated in 2011, the resort's **Boathouse Wine & Grill** is a chic staple of Phuket's fine dining scene. Nearby is the **Katathani Phuket Beach Resort** boasting a beachfront location, six pools and tennis courts.

Sunset Gazing

Come dusk, the island's southernmost extremity becomes a gathering point for drinking in the sunset as it turns the waves into a red sea of lava-like lights. At the viewpoint is a lighthouse that doubles as a museum and a shrine to the four-faced Hindu deity Brahma.

The last stop on a daytripper's big day out, now it's time to head for a sundowner and supper.

Neon Nights

After dark, most roads on Phuket lead to Patong. The bright lights and neon signs of **Patong Beach** are most mesmerizing from the comfortable terrace of the restaurant at the **Baan Yin Dee**, an excellent boutique hotel only a few minutes from the center of town. To be in the middle of the frenetic free-for-all that is **Bangla Road**, try **Patong Seafood**, now in business for more than 20 years.

Bangla is packed with beer bars, tailors, a glut of go-go bars around the U-shaped **Soi Sea Dragon**, the famous ladyboy venue **Simon Cabaret** on Soi Crocodile and the sonic-boom disco of **Banana**. The area is certainly cacophonous and a bit racy, but easy enough to avoid or use as a first-drink launching pad to explore Patong's more subdued venues, such as the **Expat Bar** in Soi Sunset or the **Vegas Thai Boxing Stadium**.

Cabaret performers, Phuket

Day 2

Start out your morning to savor the old quarter of **Phuket Town** with a breakfast special at the handsomely restored and oh-so-apropos **China Inn Café and Restaurant**. Inside, the Chinese-style shophouse also serves as an antique store. In the backyard is the restaurant, enhanced with plants, flowers and Chinese fans.

Amble around the neighborhood on a voyage of discovery rich with arts, crafts, fabrics and antiques.

On and off the roads of Dibuk, Thalang and the Phang-Nga, Sino-Colonial mansions and shophouses stand as monuments to Phuket's illustrious past as a tin-mining Mecca, populated by Chinese immigrants, with a blend of Western architectural forms and Chinese elements.

Here, you will also find significant Chinese temples like **Jui Tui**, which plays a pivotal part as a backdrop during the dramatic Vegetarian Festival. Held for nine days in late September or October, this macabre take on Taoist Lent is celebrated with processions of spirit mediums performing incredible feats of self-mortification with chains, hacksaws and walking on burning coals. It's the biggest event in Phuket city and hotel rooms are booked solid for months in advance.

Cultured Lunches

For lunch in yet more Phuket retro surrounds, hit the **Dibuk Restaurant** or **Raya House** where Thai gastronomy reigns supreme.

Close to these fine establishments is the **Sino House Phuket Hotel & Apartment** replete with the **Raintree Spa**, which makes for a rejuvenating break before hitting the road to explore the far-flung points of the island.

Next stop **Cape Panwa**, an index finger of land jutting into the Andaman Sea. Here the **Phuket Aquarium**, part of the **Phuket Marine Biological Center**, houses an exotic collection of marine creatures like sharks and lionfish, which will whet your appetite for water sports and more in-depth odysseys.

Heading east, the next bay is **Chalong**, a point of departure for many of the big game fishing trips, as well as a port for yachties thanks to the **Boat Lagoon**, Yacht Haven and **Royal Phuket Marina**.

Chyn Pracha Residence, Phuket

Late in the afternoon, this bay teems with schools of fishermen and fleets of boats setting sail or dropping anchor. Have a sundowner at one of the many inexpensive beach bars or dinner at the nautically themed **Lighthouse**, which boasts photogenic views of the harbor.

Nocturnal Spectacles

Phuket FantaSea is the number one night out for families. The ticket includes transport, a buffet dinner, entertainment and shopping spree possibilities in the cultural theme park, and a sizable show of Disney-meets-Broadway proportions with acrobats, magicians and Thai dancers.

The new upstart is **Siam Niramit Phuket**. Its modus operandi is much the same as at its Bangkok brother-in-law, combining a show melding Thai culture and history with special effects like flying angels, in addition to a shopping experience called "Village of the Four Regions". For canned culture, this is a bit on the tacky side, but cleverly constructed nonetheless.

Activities a la Carte

Phuket has such a lengthy list of activities on offer that you would need a week to even make a dent in it. Many of them, like cooking classes and diving trips, require a full day out. So for those staying longer, you can improvise a multi-day itinerary with these suggestions.

As one of the region's most crowd-pulling activities for many years now, traversing **Phang-nga Bay** in a boat and a sea canoe is a supernatural experience. Hundreds of meters tall, the limestone karsts rise out of the bay in surreal formations (see page 17).

The boat tour is the first leg, but the second part is getting into a small rubber canoe paddled by Thai guides, who head for limestone cliffs pocked with caves only accessible during low tide. These caves open into lagoons with pristine green water where the walls are edged with mangrove forests.

Many of these day trips include stopovers at the underwhelming tourist trap of **James Bond Island**.

Cooking Classes

With Thai cookery becoming one of the world's hottest cuisines both literally and figuratively, interest in classes has reached boiling point and spilled over into a number of schools, both in big hotels and private homes.

In a glut of worthy competitors, the **Phuket Thai Cookery School** is exceptionally different with open-air cooking stations on the beach. Make sure you sign up for a Friday or Saturday session that includes a tour of a fresh market. You'll learn how to whip up a few savory favorites, such as *tom yam goong* (spicy shrimp soup), *pad thai* (Thai-style noodles) and chicken with cashew nuts, then eat them with relish.

Diving

Off Phuket's eastern flank, about an hour's boat trip, are some colorful reefs for divers to immerse themselves in their natural element. Named after the innocuous leopard sharks found here, **Shark Point** attracts the most amount of aquanauts with its soft corals and sea fans, but **Anemone Reef**, the **King Cruiser wreck** and **Ko Racha Yai** are all good depending on the season and visibility.

The real sunken pleasures and natural treasures of the **Andaman Sea**, however, are found farther out in the **Surin** and **Similan Islands**, which requires doing a live aboard of a few days and nights.

EXPLORING
KO SAMUI
Exploding tourism meets
natural beauty and variety

Once the province of backpackers, who are the Marco Polos of the tourism world, much of **Ko Samui** has ascended into the upper echelons of exorbitance. Pockets of resistance are still there in the hippie holdovers of thatched bungalows on Lamai and a few other places. But areas such as the super-slick Chaweng, yacht charters and exclusive health resorts are proof positive of Samui's burgeoning appeal to the nouveau riche of China, Russia and Brazil, as well as cashed up, family-free hipsters from Europe and North America, equally prone to fits of yoga as bouts of debauchery.

About as mainstream as Thai islands get, it's been nicknamed "Costa del Samui" for its resemblance to Spain's biggest tourist area.

Chaweng

Ground zero for the big five-star resorts, fast food chains, and the most exuberant nightspots, **Chaweng** is swell for dipping a toe into Samui's ocean of attributes — and glimpsing some of its rampant over development too.

Start out the morning with a hearty Irish breakfast at **Tropical Murphy's** which will keep you going until lunch.

Using Chaweng as both a point of departure and return, it's possible to do

a reconnaissance mission of much of the island in a day by riding the ring road of 4196, and taking time out to make a few stops for sustenance of the savory kind and sightseeing.

In the northeast of the island, near the airport, your first stop should be the **Wat Phra Yai** temple. The huge 12-meter-high golden Buddha in the posture of subduing his diabolical adversary Mara is a milestone in the island's iconography.

Bang Rak

This is an especially scenic stretch of the island. Although the water is too shallow for swimming on **Bang Rak** ("Big Buddha"), the beach still fits the tropical ideal of idyllic with coconut palms holding sway and giving shade. In the morning, it's perfect for a leisurely stroll.

From here, speedboats depart to **Angthong National Marine**, reputedly the wellspring for Alex Garland's novel *The Beach*.

Most of the 40 plus islands are close to each other, making for dolphin-quick journeys (only Ko Paluay is inhabited). Tours include all sorts of swimming and snorkeling options, as well as kayaking and camping. If you visit the most precious emerald in Angthong's tiara — a

Golden Buddha at Wat Phra Yai

Ko Samui

green saltwater lake walled in by lime-stone ramparts on **Ko Mae Ko** ("Mother Island")—you can pick a leaf (quite literally) from Garland's novel.

Bo Phut

Continuing west you will arrive at **Bo Phut**. In a past life, it was a fishing village. Now it's been reincarnated as an outpost of boutique chic with a few splashes of maritime ambience. For lunch, try some grilled prawns and

squid at the **Happy Elephant**, with its sea vistas and hospitable vibe.

Seduced by Bo Phut's sleepy pace, many daytrippers end up staying here. Among the pricey, mid-sized resorts, **Anantara** is a front-runner with love-seats on each balcony and, at the beach-facing back of the property, an infinity pool overlooking the sea.

Also on Bo Phut is the **Absolute Sanctuary**, a Moroccan-accented bou-tique resort offering healthy holidays from yoga retreats to week-long detox sessions. Some of the other contenders in the growing health sector are the more spartan **Spa Resort** on Lamai, and the superlative **Kamalaya Wellness Sanctuary** on its own private beach.

Near Bo Phut are top-gear attractions for families, such as **Samui Go Kart** and the **Monkey Show**, where these agile and incredibly dextrous creatures give demonstrations of picking coconuts, the island's main cash crop.

Mae Nam

Nowhere is more emblematic of the new wave Samui than the **W Retreat** and its funky pool villas. Geographically, it's on **Mae Nam**. Aesthetically and philosophically, it's in a different league. This brand appeals to a younger crowd living healthily by day at the **Away Spa** and the first "Thaimazcal" treatment facility (based on Mexican tribal rituals that incorporate Thai ingredients), and

Na Muang Waterfall 2

partying exuberantly at nightspots like the **Woobar**, which crowns the retreat and features regular "happenings".

After a stop here for refreshments at the retreat's **TONIC Juice Bar**, it's back on the road again.

Snake Farm & Waterfalls

Rounding the western hump of the island, go through the port town of Nathon where boats depart for Ko Pha-ngan, Ko Tao and Surat Thani, and head around 15 kilometers south to the **Snake Farm**. The afternoon shows begin at 2 pm. This hour-long spectacle pits men against snakes in death-defying displays of bravado.

To cool off from the torrid, mid-afternoon meltdown, head for the **Na Muang Waterfalls** situated off the main ring road, around the halfway point between Nathon and Lamai Beach. Just beware that you will have to walk up a steep and winding trail to get there—well worth the effort for a rejuvenating dip in a jungle-surrounded pool. Kids and the young at heart will also enjoy the **Na Muang Safari Park** which offers elephant rides, monkey shows and more.

Mummified Monk

For a little detour into Samui's Twilight Zone, head to **Wat Khumaram** on Route 4169, not far from the waterfalls, to see **Luang Poh Daeng**. Since passing away in 1973, his body has barely decomposed at all, since his spiritual powers and good karma (or so his followers claim) were so developed.

Sitting upright in a glass casket, the cadaver is wearing sunglasses. Far from being a ghoulish tourist attraction, the holy man, who predicted his own death

Grandfather Rocks

and wrote out detailed instructions on how to exhibit his corpse, has been left like this to encourage the younger generation to follow Buddhist teachings.

Bound for Lamai

In the late afternoon, make tracks for the **"Grandfather and Grandmother Rocks"** (**Hin Ta** and **Hin Yai**), natural phenomena that resemble oversized genitals. They are two of the island's most photographed landmarks.

The obscene-looking rocks are close to **Lamai**, a much less frenetic alternative to Chaweng that is also home to a multitude of beach-hugging resorts and a stadium for buffalo and rooster fights.

For a stylish sundowner, check out the **Patio** at the **Pavilion Samui Boutique Resort**. If the Szechuan duck with sea scallops doesn't get you salivating, then head for Lamai's main street where you'll find a trio of excellent restaurants: the **Shamrock Pub** (with a side dish of live music), **Sala Thai** (classic local dishes) and **Barrio Latino** (Mexican and tapas).

After Dark Carousing

Lamai is quieter and far less bustling than its big sister Chaweng, and like Phuket's Patong Beach, most roads lead to Chaweng for serious partying. Nonetheless, Lamai has everything from the ubiquitous beer bars and gin palaces to music venues and even female boxing.

The legendary **Green Mango Nightclub** is the central nervous system of the island's nightlife, home to the megadisco **Reggae Pub**, many beer bars and a couple of go-go bars.

But Chaweng's after dark haunts are diverse. There's **Moulin Rouge** with cabaret shows, the sophisticated **Red Snapper** at the **Chaweng Regest Beach Resort**, the **Q Bar** disco up on the hill that boasts incredible views of the beach, and the **Ark Bar**, an old staple of the beachside fire-juggling dance scene.

For a truly exuberant and exotic night out, the can't-miss venue is **Zico's**. The all-you-can-eat Brazilian-style barbecues are to drool for and the sultry samba dancers from South America, the percussionists and DJs harmonize so perfectly with the tropical isle environs and happy-go-lucky Thai character that it's a match made in holiday heaven.

**EXPLORING
SOUTHERN THAILAND
Unparalleled natural beauty and
unique cultural traditions**

In the backwash of the 2004 tsunami that devastated the now rebuilt Khao Lak, the silver lining was that the north Andaman Sea coastline has become a greenbelt, with watersheds in eco-tourism sprouting up at Ko Rah and Ko Phra Thong, as well as breakthroughs in responsible travel and homestays. For castaway experiences, try the islands off the long and unsullied coast of Trang.

Khao Lak

One of the Andaman's top family vacation spots, **Khao Lak**, a 20-kilometer-long strip of coastal resorts, is blissfully chilled out. The beach of **Baan Niang** is small and cozy with a lovely, long strip of uncrowded sand and pristine waters. At the top end is the **Ramada** and the mega-sized **Le Meridian Khaa Lak Beach & Spa Resort**, while the family-owned **Chongfah Beach Resort** caters to the boutique set with only 30 rooms and eight beachfront bungalows.

Bang La On is the main tourist center and is a little livelier at night. Overall, it's a fairly archetypal beach town with a mouth-watering range of restaurants—seafood is usually the best choice—and a handful of Scandinavian places befitting the clientele, interspersed with travel agencies, Internet cafes, bars and souvenir shops.

In Khao Lak, swimming, sunbathing, sea gazing and getting massages on the beach are the gentle orders of torpid days. Due to the proximity of the Surin and Similan archipelagos—two of the world's top 10 dive sites—diving causes the biggest splash, with **Sea Dragon, Sea Bees, Khao Lak Scuba Adventures** and a host of other good dive shops.

While there are a handful of reefs for fun dives, most of the action is live-aboards available only during the high season from November to April.

One of the biggest events of the diving year is manta season in February and March, when these angelic creatures with two-meter wingspans swoop around the isle of **Ko Bon**. They're curious creatures that like divers and will often swim around and beside them.

But if water sports don't float your boat, other sightseeing options for daytrippers include outings to the national parks of **Khao Sok** and **Khao Lak Lam Ru** and visiting the smattering of epitaphs for tsunami victims in the form of a wave-like tunnel, a museum, a police boat and two enormous fishing vessels swept ashore and left as memorials. There is also the **Saori Foundation Center**, a workshop and crafts center that is the legacy of a Japanese monk who wanted to teach local women a skill they could use to keep their heads above water after the 10-meter-high waves inundated the coast on Boxing Day 2004.

Khao Sok National Park

Often visited on eco-centric daytrips from Khao Lak, this park is a multi-faceted diamond in the rough. Its most distinguishing features are its primeval rainforests crossed by walking trails, limestone cliffs shooting straight up

Southern Thailand

Khao Sok National Park

away under a canopy of trees, eliminating the need for air-conditioning or even fans. Solar panels power the lights. Behind the pavilion is an organic plot for carrots, onions, chili and lemongrass. This is the only bungalow operation on the island and a paragon of healthy, eco-savvy traveling, augmented by hikes and dives, at its greenest.

Ko Phra Thong

Wildlife spotting has rarely been more convenient than at the only resort on the 10-kilometer beachhead of the nearby **Ko Phra Thong**. From the terrace of any of the bungalows, sleeping 2–8 people, at the **Golden Buddha Beach Resor**t, visitors can marvel at the sight of deer, monkeys and hornbills. The undeveloped beach is also one of the last nesting sites for leatherback turtles in Thailand.

Because the North Andaman contains such wild environs, the resort also offers bird watching tours of the jungle and mangrove forests. Flying into the island's airspace and setting eyes and camera shutters aflutter is a squadron of Indian Rollers, Asian Fairy Bluebirds and Ruddy Kingfishers.

Ko Maphrao

Only eight kilometers from Phuket, **Ko Maphrao** seems a world away. Awash with folkloric traditions and old world charm, Coconut Island's locals have opened their homes and hearts to visitors who want to take in life from a real islander's perspective.

On land, the locals harvest coconuts, tap rubber trees, and make joyously colorful batik products. Visitors can also lend a hand. By sea, the locals operate the main supply lines for much of the

into the air and crowned with head-dresses of verdure, exciting caves and the rarely ruffled **Chiaw Lan Lake** dotted with floating raft houses made from latticed bamboo (electricity not included).

Other choices for staying overnight are the **Khao Sok Rainforest Resort**, which is quite basic, and the grander **Cliff & Jungle River Resort**. Both of them can arrange treks and boat trips; these are the twin engines of Khao Sok's tourist economy. Camping is possible too. As in Khao Yai National Park, in the early morning campers are sometimes awak-ened by the "mating songs" of gibbons. The male and female, who mate for life and are monogamous, sing duets every morning to mark their territory.

Ko Ra

Approaching the tiny yet mountainous island of **Ko Ra** on a long-tail boat from the **Khuraburi Pier**, as Brahminy kites swoop down to scoop fish from the water, the only part of the **Ko Ra Ecolodge** visible is a Thai-style pavilion behind a crescent of sand. All of the stylish, bamboo-latticed bungalows are tucked fresh seafood on Phuket, which means you can also help local fishermen catch spider crabs, or see how they breed lobsters and fish.

The staff of the **Agricultural Conservation Tour Club** guide visitors on walking tours or arrange mountain bikes for freewheeling around the island.

Ko Yao Noi

The Conservation Tourism Club of the **Ko Yao Noi** Community was set up to give tourists a gigantic window on the livelihoods and lifestyles of its Muslim denizens. The club's trophy case gleams with prizes for their trailblazing work, such as the World Legacy Award from *National Geographic* magazine, along with multiple accolades from the TAT for being the "Best Host" and "Best Community in Tourism".

On this island in the Andaman there are no bars or pubs. The highest structures stand no taller than the coconut palms. Bikinis are prohibited. And the environmental protocol is strict: no littering and no collecting of seashells or coral are permitted.

These caveats aside, the atmosphere on the island is relaxed and friendly. Altogether there are 30 rooms for homestays with local families. They take visitors on educational daytrips to watch the fishermen and farmers in action.

For a little more adventure, scuba diving trips around the nearby **Ko Hong-Phak Bia**, or further afield to **Ko Kai Nok** and **Krabi** province add some sea changes to landlubber itineraries.

The island is accessible by boats departing from the **Bang Rong Pier** on Phuket, the **Tha Lane Pier in Krabi**, and the **Kuraburi Pier** in Phang-Nga province.

Trang

Experiencing a small groundswell of newfound popularity are several of the 46 islands off this 800-kilometer-long coast that contains some of the most secret nooks and crannies on the country's map. None of the islands have five-star facilities, or much in the way of shopping and nightlife, but if you're looking for a more castaway kind of experience, this area is just the ticket.

Ko Kradan is one of the most beautiful and idyllic of Trang's islands with angel's hair beach. It's also renowned as the site of the annual "Underwater Weddings" where couples take the plunge dressed in scuba gear. It's accessed by boats (every 1.5 hours) from **Pak Meng Pier**.

Ko Libong is the biggest of the bunch and something of a nest of bird watchers. Near the Libong Beach Resort are reefs for snorkelers.

This Muslim island is also a floating home to the endangered dugong or "sea cow", whereas **Ko Ngai** and **Ko Mook** are studies in opposites: the former is tiny and the latter is huge, mountainous and contains the famous "Emerald Cave".

Ko Lipe

The villagers and boatmen of **Ko Lipe** are predominantly sea gypsies. Most of the staff working at the bungalow outfits are southern Thai Muslims or Buddhists, and you'll often overhear conversations in Malay. Indeed, this remote island, some seven kilometers from the nautical border with Malaysia, is a stew of different cultures and ethnicities. That accounts for part of its charm. The rest comes from the fact that because Ko Lipe is not very accessible during most of the monsoon season, from May to October, the island has been environmentally protected from the more adverse side effects of herd-driven tourism.

That said, there are some changes in the offing and bigger resorts going up, such as the grand **Serendipity Beach Resort** on **Sunrise Beach** (the Big Lebowski suite has especially good views), as well as the swanky **Hammam Beach Resort & Spa**.

Ko Lipe is part of the **Tarutao National Marine Park**, where the original *Survivor* series was shot. Only **Ko Tarutao** (a former penal colony) and **Ko Adang** have accommodations in the form of government-built bungalows.

Every morning and afternoon during the high and dry season, from November to May, ferries and speedboats depart from the **Pak Bara Pier** in Satun province, which is about 90 minutes by minibus from the railway station or the airport in Had Yai.

Andaman Discoveries

After Bodhi Garrett, an American born in Kathmandu, had his job at the Golden Buddha Beach Resort, and all his belongings, swept away by the 2004 tsunami, he started programs to equip locals who had lost their livelihoods with new skills in computers, English and guiding tours.

That was the genesis of Andaman Discoveries. The Kuiburi-based tour operator in Phang-Nga province has gone on to win many major laurels, such as Virgin's Responsible Tourism Award for Conservation of Cultural Heritage, in tribute to their community-based itineraries, homestays and nature jaunts.

The "voluntourist experiences" they offer, like teaching English to children, fishing, farming and planting trees are life-altering journeys, many travelers say, providing a level of cultural and familial immersion impossible on a more superficial and escapist vacation.

Ko Lipe

EXPLORING THE GREAT NORTHEAST
Ancient Khmer monuments and famous hospitality

L ess than 10 percent of the arrivals who descend in droves on Thailand make it to the Northeast. That's a shame. The kingdom's largest region has much to recommend it: temples of Khmer vintage and antiquity; Mekong-straddling towns and maritime odysseys; spicy dishes to tantalize the taste buds; and incredibly friendly locals.

But there are a few drawbacks too. The bigger urban centers are a bit drab and host little nightlife, English is not that widely spoken, and some of the rural roads are in a state of disrepair.

But do not let these speed bumps get in the way of exploring the country's most unexplored region. You'll need about a week to do the following itinerary, though it's been designed so you can start in any place, or if you're coming from Laos or northern Thailand do it in reverse.

Nakhon Ratchasima

Sometimes referred to as Khorat, this city on the **Khorat Plateau** is about three hours northeast of the capital. It's a sprawling city of a quarter million inhabitants well served by buses and trains from Bangkok. For an overnighter, book a room at the **Hermitage Resort**, a mid-range hotel with a good spa and Chinese Restaurant. The hotel's karaoke

bar will give you an earful of the northeast's biggest night out.

The city is a jumping off point for **Khao Yai National Park** and the dude ranch of **Pensuk Great Western**, which ropes in city slickers with cowboys, horses and Wild East trappings.

Renowned for producing popular dairy products, the **Chokchai Farm** milks the cash cow of agro-tourism on weekends and official holidays. That's when visitors come to learn all about life on a dairy farm. The steakhouse, which has several branches in Bangkok, is excellent too.

Phimai Historical Park

Situated some 60 kilometers from the capital of Nakhon Ratchasima, in the town of **Phimai**, is this former outpost for the empire builders of Angkor. In fact, some of these well-preserved structures in the historical park are thought to be older than parts of Angkor Wat.

Phimai Historical Park

Dating from the tumultuous turn of the 11th century, the centerpiece, **Prasat Hin Phimai**, is the most colossal sandstone sanctuary in Thailand. It is also the park's focal point.

Land of the Dinosaurs

For those fascinated by reptiles and dinosaurs—and what boy isn't?—taking a detour due north to the provincial capital of **Khon Kaen** is the real reptilian deal.

Ironically, the business and higher learning capital of the Northeast is situated in the midst of the region's biggest dinosaur graveyard. A few skeletal specimens from here, first discovered in Thailand back in 1976, are on display in the **Phu Wiang Dinosaur Museum**. The museum is on the grounds of **Phu Wiang National Park**. The park's excavation pits show where some of these primeval monsters (several discovered only in Thailand) were unearthed.

For a full day out, combine the park and museum with a visit to **Ban Kok Sa-Nga** ("Cobra Village"), where locals raise and put on snake shows beside the temple, and **Ban Kok Tortoise Town**, where hundreds of sacred tortoises trudge through the streets, backyards and even the homes of the inhabitants, as they are treated like sacred cows in India. Both hamlets are about 50 kilometers outside of the capital and are well sign posted.

Buri Ram

Buri Ram means "Pleasant Town". Not a place that strains for superlatives, this humble and unpretentious hamlet is the jumping-off point for the phenomenal **Wat Khao Phnom Ruang**. Perched on a clifftop that affords heart-stopping

vistas of the verdant countryside, this temple devoted to Shiva, where a stone phallic symbol remains a sexual object of veneration, is both massive and remarkably intact. After a morning spent touring the temple, it's off for some wild times in the country's capital of elephants.

Surin

Just down the road from **Buri Ram**, also on the main railway line, is this crossroads where Lao, Khmer, Thai and Kui cultures converge; the provincial seal is the Hindu god Indra riding a sacred elephant before a Khmer-style shrine. That sets the stage for **Surin**'s main act—a village where elephants are treated like members of the family. At **Baan Ta Klang**, many visitors do a homestay, learning to eat, sleep and live like locals.

At the **Elephant Study Center**, there are circus-like daily shows and elephant rides. For voluntourists, the new Surin Project is a spin-off of the Elephant Nature Foundation run by the famous conservationist Sangduen "Lek" Chailert. The project requires paid volunteers to help with their new facilities for abused and abandoned tuskers, participating in basic elephant care.

Elephant line-up at Surin

Mekong Odysseys

As Southeast Asia's biggest bloodline of commerce and culture, the **Mekong River** feeds and waters hundreds of coastal communities.

To tap this rich vein of history and sights for city-sore eyes, make your way up the porous border with Laos through **Ubon Ratchathani** and **Yasothon**, where visitors have a blast at the annual **Rocket Festival**, to the eponymous capital of **Nakhon Phanom** province. It's a sleepy city with a violent past thanks to its proximity to Laos during the Vietnam War. Between the capital and the airbase is **Ban Nachok**, the village in which Ho Chi Minh took refuge for three years. The Vietnamese leader's former residence doubles as a museum celebrating his revolutionary life.

The province's other main attraction is **Wat Phra That Phanom**, the region's oldest and grandest temple, located some 50 kilometers south of here in the town of **That Phanom**.

Use the **Nakhon Phanom River View Hotel** in the provincial capital as a base of explorations. The semi-alfresco restaurant comes complete with gorgeous views of the Mekong.

Wat Phra That Phanom

Nong Khai

For soaking up more of the waterway's maritime ambience, this is Thailand's Loch Ness, though part of the mystery it harbors is exposed during the **Naga Fireball Festival** held every October on the last night of Buddhist Lent, when orbs of light mysteriously rise from the river, arc hundreds of meters through the sky and promptly disappear. The pious attribute them to Naga, the seven-headed Serpent Lord whose body and crested heads forms the balustrades of temples. In one tale, these dragon-like creatures dwell at the bottom of the Mekong River. To pay homage to the Buddha every year, they shoot off the fireballs. A more scientific explanation is that the orbs come from methane deposits ignited every year by the full moon.

Whatever you believe, you can still soak up some of the city's maritime magic at the legendary **Mut Mee Guesthouse**. It's got rooms with Thai decorations overlooking the Mekong, a garden with hammocks, a good bar-cum-restaurant and warmhearted staff. They also have yoga classes and massages.

In these parts, a paramount pleasure is renting a bicycle from the guesthouse to explore some of the riverside roads and the surreal sculpture garden called the **Pavilion of Kaewkoo**. Designed by a semi-mad mystic of Lao ethnicity who claimed to be "half man and half snake", the mummified remains of Luang Poo Boun Leua Sourirat are encased in glass on the third floor of the main building. All in all, the garden of Bosch-like grotesques and beatific deities contains around 100 sculptures, many based on the Buddhist and Hindu canons. Some of them are 20–25 meters high.

Among gourmands, Nong Khai is also reputed to have one of the country's best Vietnamese restaurants, **Daeng Namnuang**, serving up delights like pork spring rolls at a riverside venue.

Yet another local speciality is the sunset and dinner cruises. Mut Mee's boat, the *Nagarina*, is a reliable choice. Unlike some of the tasteless versions of Thai fare the major hotel cruises offer on Bangkok cruises, this onboard meal, heavy on freshly caught fish, is the real McCoy.

Chiang Khan

After a night or two in Nong Khai, it's time for a gentle drive to **Chiang Khan**, a rustic town on the Mekong in the mountainous province of **Loei** that epitomizes the "slow travel" trend. On the main drag you'll find a photogenic selection of old wooden homes, shops

Phi Ta Khon

and inexpensive guesthouses, and life set to a sleepwalker's pace.

The **Chiang Khan Guesthouse** is an old teak house enhanced with lovely river views to gorge your eyes on those cotton candy pink and fireball orange sunrises and sunsets. Run by a Dutchman and his Thai wife, who are treasure chests of information, they will arrange everything from rafting trips and cooking classes to performances of local music and side trips to the famous **Chateau de Loei** winery. In the guesthouse's superb restaurant, make sure you fill up on those staples of Lao and Isaan food: papaya salad, barbecued chicken, sticky rice and spicy catfish.

Loei

For Thais, the province's most popular attraction is the **Phu Kradeung National Park**. The bell-shaped mountain is named after its centerpiece. Hardier visitors hike to the pinnacle where there's a camping ground with tents to rent. It makes for a wonderful overnighter.

During the day, there are 50 kilometers of walking trails to explore. At night, alpine breezes provide refreshment and the stars are rhinestones studded on a black velvet sky.

For foreigners, however, Loei's main event is the **Phi Ta Khon** ("Ghosts with Human Eyes") Festival held every June or July, when young men wearing colorful, ghoulish masks and waving enormous phallic symbols around take over the streets of the town of **Dansai**, where old men dress up as ladyboys and traditional dancers parade and pirouette through the streets during the reenactment of a Buddhist folk tale in which the sacred and profane do a mating dance.

AUTHOR'S RECOMMENDATIONS

Any country as well developed and visitor friendly as Thailand offers a mind-boggling array of activities, hotels, restaurants, accommodations, etc. By listing the crème de la crème, the author hopes that his hard-won experiences will help you to whittle down your choices.

Top Hotels and Resorts

Bangkok—Arun Residence; Dream Hotel; Ibis Bangkok Riverside; Old Bangkok Inn; Mandarin Oriental Hotel; Sheraton Grande Sukhumvit; Shangri-la Hotel; Sofitel Bangkok; St. Regis; Siam Kempinski

Chiang Mai—Dusit D2; At Niman; Four Seasons Resort; Kantary Hills; Mandarin Oriental Dhara Devi; Rachamankha; The Chedi; U Chiang Mai Resort

Phuket—Amanpuri; Indigo Pearl; Le Meridien Phuket Beach Resort; Mom Tri's Villa Royale; Sala Resort & Spa; Six Senses Hideaway Yao Noi; Twinpalms Phuket

Best Foods & Restaurants

Bangkok—Bo.lan; Face; Flying Chicken Restaurant; Four Seasons Sunday Brunch; Hemlock; Lord Jim's; Nahm; Napa on 26; Soul Food Mahanakorn

Chiang Mai—Heun Phen; Le Grand Lanna; Moxie; The Riverside; W by Wanlamun

Ko Samui—Bang Po Seafood; Dining on the Rocks; Spirit House; Zico's

Phuket—Baan Rim Pa; Mom Tri's Boathouse Wine & Grill; Black Ginger; Kan Eang@pier; Siam Supper Club

Best Shopping

Bangkok—Chatuchak Market; Khaosan Road; Jewelry Trade Center; Jim Thompson Shop; Lotus Arts de Vivre; Pak Khlong Flower Shop; Gaysorn Plaza; Mansion 7; The Emporium

Chiang Mai—Ban Tawai; Central Airport Plaza; Night Bazaar; Sunday Walking Street; Thai Silk Village

Ko Samui—Beach Road; Classic Gems; Naga Pearl Farm; Trend Fashion

Phuket—Central Festival Phuket; Chai Batik; Chan's Antiques; Island Furniture

Hippest Nightspots

Bangkok—Hemingway's; Iron Fairies; Long Table; Phranakorn Bar; Q Bar; Saxophone

Chiang Mai—Darling Wine Pub; The Pub; Kalare Food Court; Mix Bar; Silapa Thai Lounge & Bar; Rachamankha

Ko Samui—Ark Bar; Karma Sutra; Q Bar; Green Mango Soi; W Retreat

Phuket—DiVine; Simon Cabaret; Stereo Lab; Vanilla Sky Bar & Lounge

Best Sporting Activities, Hikes & Eco-Trips

Sporting Activities—Scuba Diving; Mountain Biking; Golfing; Muay Thai; Rock Climbing; Big Game Fishing; Whitewater Rafting

Homestays and Agro-Tourism

Eco Adventures—Hiking in Kaeng Krachan National Park; Bird Watching on Doi Suthep; Cycling in Sukhothai; Diving in Ko Tao

Kid-friendly Activities

Angthong National Marine Park

ATV Tours in Phuket

Crocodile Farm

Dream World

Dusit Zoo

Night Safari

Phuket Fantasea

Samui Go-Kart

Siam Ocean World

Siam Niramit

Siam Park City

Best Temples & Museums

Ayutthaya—Wat Sri San Phet

Bangkok—Royal Barges Museum; Wat Arun; Rattanakosin Exhibition Hall; Jim Thompson House; Wimanmek Mansion; Forensic Medicine Museum

Buri Ram—Phnom Ruang Historical Park

Chiang Mai—Wat Chedi Luang; Wat Chiang Men; Wat Phra Singh; Wat Lok Moli

Chiang Rai—Wat Rong Khun

Ko Samui—Big Buddha

Phuket—Phuket Seashell Museum; Wat Chalong

Samut Prakan Province—Ancient City

Sukhothai—Wat Mahathat

Best Spas & Health Retreats

Bangkok—Dahra Beauty & Spa; Devarana Spa; Spa Botanica; Elemis; TRIA Integrative Wellness Center

Ko Samui—Absolute Sanctuary; Banyan Tree Spa Samui; Kamalaya Wellness Sanctuary; Tamarind Springs

Chiang Mai—Dheva Spa; Cheeva Spa; Green Bamboo Massage; Oasis Spa Lanna; Tao Garden Health Spa and Resort

Hua Hin—The Barai; Chiva-Som International Health Resort

Phuket—Abbysan Yoga & Wellness Center; Atmanjai Wellness Center; Thanyapura Sports and Leisure Club; Paresa Spa; Six Senses Evason

THAILAND'S TOP HOTELS & RESORTS

From boutique chic to five-star grandeur and a few mid-range choices too

Few countries in the world offer such an abundance of accommodations for such affordable rates. From humble guesthouses to one-off boutique hotels with only a few rooms to opulent suites in luxury international chain hotels, there is loads of room to choose. Because Bangkok has seen such an oversupply of rooms, it does keep the rates down. Boutique hotels, in particular, are sprouting up all over the country, while the budget hotel sector such as Accor's Ibis brand is gaining ground.

Room rates in Thailand, especially Bangkok, can vary significantly between different seasons. During the high season from November to May, rooms can be 20–50 percent more than during the rainy season. From December 15 to January 15 — often called the "peak season" — many hotels and resorts charge peak rates and reservations are essential. For longer stays of a week or more, check out the many "serviced apartments," which have all the amenities and cleaning services of a real hotel but offer better discounts. Booking online can also result in sweet deals.

BANGKOK

Arun Residence
There are only five rooms in this 70-year-old Sino-Colonial mansion, which is blessed with views of the Chao Phraya River and the Temple of Dawn. All done up in wood and creamy shades, the rooms are modernized with DVDs and mini-bars. Definitely book ahead.
36-38 Soi Pratoo Nok Yoong, Maharat Road, +66 (0)2 221 9158, www. arunresidence.com

Dream Hotel
The most internationally applauded of the city's newer accommodations, the Dream, true to its name, is a surreal combination of exotica and Western creature comforts. They call it a "fashion hotel", and being on a super-model's salary would certainly help to enjoy it more.
10 Sukhumvit Soi 15, +66 (0)2 254 8500, www.dreambkk.com

Ibis Bangkok Riverside
In the burgeoning budget sector, this is the best of the bunch. Conveniently located close to the river taxis and with a free shuttle bus to the BTS, the Ibis makes a good home base for exploring the capital.
27 Soi Charoe Nakhon 17 Charoen Nakhon Road, +66 (0)2 659 2888, www.ibishotel.com

Old Bangkok Inn
Each of the 10 rooms in this boutique hotel has been furnished with golden teak, hand-painted ceramics and equipped with PCs and broadband. Close to Khaosan Road and the Grand Palace area of historic attractions.
607 Phra Sumen Road, +66 (0)2 629 1787, www.oldbangkokinn.com

Author's Lounge, Mandarin Oriental Hotel

Mandarin Oriental Hotel

The grande dame of hotels in Thailand has lost none of her luster or colonial charm. The Author's Wing of suites devoted to famous writers like Joseph Conrad and Somerset Maugham is particularly sumptuous, and the seafood restaurant Lord Jim's and the live jazz venue the Bamboo Bar are splendidly entertaining.
48 Charoenkrung Soi 38, +66 (0)2 659 9000, www.mandarinoriental.com/ bangkok

Sheraton Grande Sukhumvit

The deluxe rooms in this rarefied five-star are all Thai silk, marble and teakwood. Another bonus is the Living Room lounge with live jazz seven nights a week and unrivaled benefits at the Grande Spa.
250 Sukhumvit Road, +66 (0)2 649 8888, www.sheratongrandesukhmvit.com

Shangri-la Hotel

The two-winged riverfront hotel has spacious and opulent rooms. In the slightly pricier Krungthep Wing, guests have personal butlers. Also available in this wing are serviced apartments discounted for longer stays.

89 Soi Suan Wat Plu, off Charoenkrung Road, +66 (0)2 236 7777, www.shangri-la.com

Sofitel Bangkok

All the dabs and splashes of local color, like wooden floors and Thai silks, lend these rooms a warm, artistic flair; and their specially designed beds are some of the comfiest and roomiest around. Three superb restaurants serve French, Cantonese and Mediterranean fare.
288 Silom Road, +66 (0)2 238 1991, www.sofitel.com

St. Regis

Opened in 2011, this timelessly elegant hotel has already notched up a number of firsts: the first St. Regis property in Southeast Asia; the first hotel where each guest has their own concierge; and it's got the first Elemis spa (a British brand) in Thailand.
St. Regis Bangkok, 159 Thanon Ratchadamri, +66 (0)2 207 7777, www.bangkok.com/the-st-regis-bangkok/

St. Regis

Siam Kempinski

Right beside Southeast Asia's biggest luxury mall, Siam Paragon, this new hotel redefines luxury, boasting a wide selection of rooms and suites, including the Cabana Rooms and 98 serviced residences. The Brasserie Europa is also winning hearts and stomachs with its buffet breakfasts, and Sra Bua by Kiin Kiin serves Thai fusion dishes in an upscale setting.

991/9 Rama I Road, +66 (0)2 162 9000, www.kempinski.com

CHIANG MAI

Dusit D2

Contemporary Thai design just got a funky facelift at this boutique hotel. With a sumptuous spa, well-equipped health club and comprehensive meeting facilities, this is a good all-round bet. The location right in the pumping heart of the Night Bazaar is another plus.

100 Chang Klan Road, +66 (0)5 399 9999, www.dusit.com/dusit-d2

At Niman

This boutique property with nine utterly unique rooms (all based on Himalayan cultures) typifies the arty spirit of Chiang Mai, and it's fittingly located in amongst the galleries and shops around Walking Street. Loads of little extras like free bicycles for guests to use and northern-style breakfasts complement the free-spirited vibe.

37 Nimmanhemin Road, Soi 9, +66 (0)5 322 4949, www.atnimancm.com

Four Seasons Resort

Talk about getting away from it all. This resort, boasting northern-style pavilions and teak-made pool villas replete with vistas of mountains and rice terraces, is about as classically Thai as resorts get. It's also got a great little cooking school and it's only about five minutes' drive from the Summit Green Valley Country Club. Package deals for families are worth looking into.

Mae Rim-Samoeng Old Road, +66 (0)5 329 8181, www.fourseasons.com/ chiangmai

Kantary Hills

These one- and two-bedroom serviced apartments are an excellent choice for families or a group of friends. Situated on the outskirts of Chiang Mai, the rooms are built around a pool and have mountain vistas sure to spellbind. All the apartments have washing machines too.

44/1-2 Nimmanhaemin Road, Soi 12, +66 (0)5 322 2111, www.kantarygroup.com

Mandarin Oriental Dhara Devi

Sprawling across 60 gorgeously landscaped acres set around terraced paddy

Mandarin Oriental Dhara Devi, colonial suite

fields, this resort is an ancient Lanna village full of architectural wonders, wooden pavilions, and period piece archways, set off against accommodations with acclaimed restaurants and an outstanding spa. The 123 villas, colonial suites and residences make for good family getaways.

51/4 Chiang Mai–Sankampaeng Road, +66 (0)5 388 8888, www.mandarinoriental.com/chiangmai

Rachamankha

Owned and operated by a Thai architect whose pedigree shows in the attention to detail and beautiful layout of this Lanna-style hotel. Spread over a hectare but with only 20-odd rooms and two suites guarantees a tranquil retreat. It's also close to all the attractions in the old part of town.

6 Rachamankha Soi 9, +66 (0)5 390 4111-3, www.rachamankha.com

The Chedi

For those in search of riverside ambience, this five-star sanctuary will make a big splash. Embellished with contemporary design smarts wrought in classically Thai motifs, these rooms and suites have incredible views of the Ping River. A good array of F&B outlets is complemented by the Terrace Bar and Cigar Lounge. Work out those holiday guilt pangs of self-indulgence at the high-tech gym.

123 Charoen Prathet Road, 66 (0)5 325 3333, www.ghmhotels.com

U Chiang Mai Resort

A four-star bonanza for boutique travelers in the middle of the old town, this hotel has an incredible range of bespoke services, a 24-hour gym, "breakfast whenever and wherever" and free yoga classes a couple of times a week. The warmth of the hospitality is only matched by the warm earthy tones of the rooms and décor.

70 Ratchadamnoen Road, www.uhotels resorts.com

PHUKET

Amanpuri

For beach goers in search of sun, sand and serenity, this fabulous hotel with what amounts to its own private beach, should sate all of those hungers, for a princely price though. Considering the tennis courts, yoga classes, on-site restaurants and bars, guests never have to leave this Thai-accented resort, but usually end up taking the resort's luxury yacht charters.

Pansea Beach, +66 (0)7 632 4333, www. amanresorts.com

Indigo Pearl

The extravagant resort has scooped most of the top travel magazine awards for its utterly original mélange of industrial chic and Phuket's tin-mining past. The choice of accommodations is mind-boggling, from the new D-Buk Suites for families to private pool villas and the Pearl Shell Suites (all completely different and each with a personal butler.)

Nai Yang Beach and National Park, +66 (0)7 632 7006, www.indigo-pearl.com

Le Meridien Phuket Beach Resort

This massive seaward-facing resort is one of the standard-setters on Karon. It's probably best for families, because it's got plenty of pools and mini-golf and other water sports on offer. The private beach setting is another very big pro.

29 Soi Karon Nui, +66 (0)7 637 0100, www.starwoodhotels.com

Mom Tri's Villa Royale

The owner's pedigree as an artist and descendant is on picturesque display in this luxurious boutique property and spa overlooking the beach of Kata Noi. Choose from 10 different kinds of suites, and expect royal treatment from staff.
12 Kata Noi Road, Kata Noi Beach, +66 (0)7 633 3568, www.villaroyalephuket.com

Sala Resort & Spa

For that Robinson Crusoe feeling of splendid isolation, Mai Khao Beach is the way to go and this is the place to stay for visitors with deep pockets. The pool villas are an enormous 167 square meters, the one-bedroom units much bigger. Beautiful grounds with three outdoor pools and water lily ponds completes the picture. The resort also organizes very good tours and elephant treks.
333 Moo 3 Mai Khao Beach, +66 (0)7 633 8888, www.salaresorts.com/phuket

Six Senses Hideaway Yao Noi

Equidistant between Phuket and Krabi, Ko Yao is an impeccable, predominantly Muslim island. This resort is the pinnacle of fine eco-savvy living with a choice of pool villas within gawking distance of the limestone karsts of Phang-Nga Bay. Great departure point for island-hopping odysseys too.
56 Moo 5, Ko Yao Noi, +66 (0)7 641 8500, www.sixsenses.com

Twinpalms Phuket

The Grand Deluxe Lagoon Pool Rooms are surrounded by tropical gardens, providing that necessary juxtaposition between urbanity and nature, as is the scenic location on Surin Beach but only a 15-minute drive from Patong. The penthouses and duplex suites with high-tech trappings deliver that wow factor.
06/46 Moo 3, Surin Beach Road, www.twinpalms-phuket.com

KO SAMUI

Bundhari Spa Resort & Villas Samui

A gently sloping hill is the idyllic setting for these immaculately appointed accommodations. Located outside the clamorous Party Central of Chaweng, which is visible in the distance, this bay straddling resort has an array of accommodations in the Southern Thai style.
111/1 Moo 5, Chaweng Beach, +66 (0)7 791 5000, www.centarahotelsresorts.com

Kamalaya

In the wellness stakes on Samui, this sanctuary is the front runner. Hugging the southeast coastline, the resort was built around a cave that was once used by Buddhist monks as a meditation retreat. The natural setting makes these

Kamalaya

programs to cure stress and lose weight, to fast and detox, to get acupuncture and massages, all the healthier. There is also a delicious menu of organic fare and a staff made up of Western doctors, naturopaths and yoga teachers.
102/9 Moo 3, Laem Set Road, +66 (0)7 742 9800, www.kamalaya.com

Mae Nam Resort

If you're in search of a mid-range resort with a nice beachside location and big bungalows, look no farther. The Family Rooms are excellent value and, remarkably enough, none of the accommodations go up much in the high season. Another big bonus is that peace and quietude reign on this blonde stretch of sand.
1/3 Moo 4, Mae Nam Beach, +66 (0)7 724 7286-7, maenamresort.com

Santiburi Golf Resort & Spa

For action-oriented couples and families this phenomenally designed resort is on par with Samui's finest. Take your pick from golf, water sports, Thai boxing, football and squash. There is also an activity center for kids. The villas are arranged in the jungle-like environs for maximum privacy and the beautiful tout-free beach is restricted to hotel guests.
12/12 Moo 1, Maenam Beach, +66 (0)7 742 5031-5, www.santiburi.com

W Retreat

This resort typifies the new wave of Samui and its hip young moneyed clientele. Occupying a prime chunk of real estate on the side of the mountain, these chic pool villas have awe-arousing sea views. The Away Spa with the TONIC juice bar and the Thaimazcal treatment facility (based on Mexican tribal rituals that incorporate Thai ingredients), and the alfresco Woobar serving as the property's party hat is a quartet of healthy debauchery.
4/1 Moo 1 Tambol Maenam, Mae Nam, +66 (0)7 791 5999

W Retreat

THAILAND'S BEST FOODS & RESTAURANTS
Eat your way around the country with this savory selection

One of the world's greatest foodie cities with one of the most brilliant cuisines, Thailand is a movable feast with a cornucopia of dishes catering to all budgets.

BANGKOK

Bo.lan
This small, trendy and expensive eatery appeals to those taste buds burned out on typical Thai dishes like spicy prawn soup. The "Bo.lan Balance Menu" is a virtual guide to how Thais order dinner, combining all the five major tastes and flavors, from a Thai salad (*yum*) to a curry and soup. It's part of the slow food movement, using all organic ingredients and freshly made dishes, so don't complain about the slow service. Reservations essential.
42 Soi Pichai Ronnarong, Sukhumvit Soi 26 Road, +66 (0)2 260 2962, www.bolan.co.th

Face
Rare is the bar that can combine museum quality artefacts with congenial service and primo food, but that's exactly the hat trick which Face consistently scores. Not only can diners gorge themselves on authentic Thai, Indian and Japanese dishes, but the artworks, wood carvings and Siamese iconography provide a feast for thought and artistic reflection.
29 Sukhumvit Road Soi 38, +66 (0)2 713 6048, www.facebars.com

Flying Chicken Restaurant
You haven't really dined out until you've seen your chicken dinner shot out of a catapult and caught by a waiter on his spiked helmet as he pedals a unicycle. Truly a bizarre night out, and worth bragging about with pics on Facebook, this inexpensive novelty restaurant is close to the new Bang Na skytrain station on the Bearing line.
99/1 Bangna Trad, opposite Royal Dragon and BITEC, +66 (0)2 399 5252

Four Seasons Sunday Brunch
Sunday brunch has been the flavor of the last few years in Bangkok's big hotels, but nobody does it up in such grand style as the Four Seasons. Four of the hotel's restaurants team up to provide a mouth-watering buffet with everything from Japanese to Italian and tiger prawns to roast duck. Book ahead.
155 Rajadamri Road, +66 (0)2 126 8866, www.fourseasons.com/bangkok

Hemlock
The pioneer of all the artsy bars on the Phra Arthit strip, just off the river and near Khaosan Road, Hemlock features a menu of ancient and royal dishes difficult to find elsewhere, such as *khao hor bai bua* (flavored jasmine rice and lotus seed stuffed with prawns, pork and fried Chinese sausage). It's a small, intimate place with Thai art on the walls and jazz standards on the sound system. Very reasonable prices and a good wine list.
56 Thanon Phra Arthit, Banglamphu, +66 (0)2 282 7507

Lord Jim's

Named after the Joseph Conrad novel of adventure on the high seas, this seafood specialist offers fantastic buffet lunches. All the fresh sashimi and lobster and foie de gras you could ever hope to stuff back in one sitting. The selection of desserts will give anyone a sweet tooth. For maximum maritime ambience, get a table by the river.

48 Oriental Avenue, +66 (0)2 659 9000 Ext. 7680-1, www.mandarinoriental.com

Napa on 26

Napa on 26

Possibly the capital's most well-kept secret on the dining scene, Napa is a study in subdued elegance serving five-star food for three-star prices. Signature dishes like "pan fried snow fish on white bean puree with pink grapefruit beurre blanc" are done to perfection. The set lunches are great value for money and there's a lengthy wine list available for iPads.

115 Soi Sukhumvit 26, Nihonmachi 2 floor, behind K Village, +66 (0)2 258 2622, www.napaon26.com

Nahm

The first Thai restaurant in the world awarded a Michelin star, this is the spin-off from its home base in London. Located in the urbane Metropolitan Hotel, this stylish eatery seeks to revive age-old recipes and forgotten dishes such as "jungle curry with freshwater fish". It's pricey and the wine is stratospheric so consider the set menu. Also note that Nahm is only open 7 pm–11 pm.

27 South Sathorn Road, +66 (0)2 625 3412, www.comohotels.com

Nahm

Khao soi mieng kham

Soul Food Mahanakorn

The threefold mantra for this newish restaurant is "Good ingredients. Honest cooking. Serious drinks." Housed in a refurbished three-story shophouse near the Thonglor BTS, the restaurant's version of local "soul food" is dishes such as *khao soi mieng kham* (northern noodles), a Burmese-style pork curry, or fresh sea bass stuffed with spices and grilled inside a green banana leaf. Organic rice (white, brown or red) makes for a healthy side dish. All cocktails are double strength.
56/10 Sukhumvit Soi 55, +66 (0)2 714 7708, www.soulfoodmahanakorn.com

CHIANG MAI

Heun Phen

For a great dining experience head where many locals go, like here, an inexpensive restaurant serving up authentic northern Thai food in a venue that could be an antiques shop. To get a good sampler of northern dishes, order the *khantoke* dinner set. For lunch try the *khao soi* noodle buffet.
112 Rachamankha Rd, +66 (0)5 381 4548

Le Grand Lanna

This garden setting adds a whole lot more natural and tropical allure to fine dining. Located in the palatial Mandarin Oriental Dhara Dhevi, the restaurant has some brilliant signature dishes like "Soft shell crab salad with spicy green mango and mint leaves" and "Northern Thai

curry with pork and pickled garlic". Make sure you catch the traditional dance show every night at 8 pm.
51/4 Sankampaeng Road Moo 1, +66 (0)5 388 8888 Ext. 8566

Moxie

For a splurge in a funky, hipper-than-thou atmosphere, this restaurant in the Dusit D2 hotel fits the bill. Thai fusion dishes like "Spaghetti with Chiang Mai Sausage" and "Baked Baby Pork Ribs" are the mainstays of the menu, and recently they've added organic coffee from the nearby Doi Chaang project. Rarely crowded, it's good for a quiet night out.
100 Chang Klan Road, +66 (0)5 399 9999, www.dusit.com

The Riverside

This old favorite is still rocking. Easily one of the liveliest atmospheres in the city thanks to a festive crowd and live music every night. Plus the menu is extensive for both Thai and Western dishes, and vegetarians are catered for too with a sweet green curry full of tofu and veggies. The setting on the Ping River is another bonus.
9-11 Charoenrat Road, +66 (0)5 324 3239, www.theriversidechiangmai.com

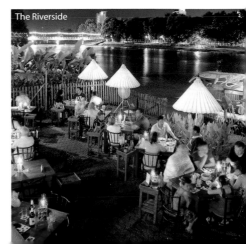
The Riverside

W by Wanlamun

This place is quite the mélange: an outdoor setting in a garden terrace with gourmet Thai fare, fusion dishes and a wonderful selection of classically French pastries. In particular, the fish curry custard baked in a banana leaf is heavenly. Throw in all the extras like fine china, tablecloths and good service and it's worth the extra money.
1 Chang Moi Rd. Soi 2, +66 (0)5 323 2328, www.wanlamun.com

KO SAMUI

Bang Po Seafood

Serving seafood so fresh it's only just stopped squirming, this inexpensive Thai-style eatery is so close to the beach you can smell the sea spray. Tuck into a steamed fish with lemon or the grilled squid or the baby octopus soup or a catfish curry, they're all good and at a fraction of the price you'll pay in the more touristy restaurants.
56/4 Moo 6, Mae Nam Beach, +66 (0)7 742 0010

Dining on the Rocks

This restaurant gets our vote for the most breath-robbing views and original ambience on the island. At the Six Senses Resort, they built 10 terraced decks that offer both alfresco and covered dining, along with a 270-degree panorama of the islands and sea. The food is equally original with "New Asian Cuisine" and "Modern Interpretative Cuisine". An extensive wine list and two other bars on the rocks ensure that this is a great place to linger for a drink or five. All in all, it's an expensive yet memorable meal out.
9/10 Moo 5, Bo Phut, +66 (0)7 724 5678, www.sixsenses.com

Spirit House

This is not just a restaurant—it's a magical realm of fairy lights, mythical icons, Siamese folklore, lotus ponds and temple-style architecture. For highly recommended signature dishes, there's the red duck curry with tomatoes, lychees and grapes, or the hearty Massaman curry with potatoes and peanuts. Upstairs, they've got *khan toke*, banquet-style dinners accompanied by Thai dancers and tunes.
155/60 Moo 2, Chaweng, +66 (0)7 741 4101, www.spirithousesamui.com

Zico's

When tiring of noodles and rice, this Brazilian-style restaurant is a welcome taste-changer. Starring an all-you-can-stuff-down barbecue done Brazilian style with green and red signs for stop and go, combined with an extensive salad bar that is complemented by sexy samba queens and a live band laying down salsa grooves. The dance shows begin at 8 pm and continue every hour until the grand finale at 11 pm.
38/2 Moo 3, Chaweng, +66 (0)7 723 1560-3, www.zicossamui.com/restaurant.asp

PHUKET

Baan Rim Pa

Frequented by the local community and international jet set alike (make sure to check out the photograph of a bronzed Kate Moss near the entrance), the menu features "Royal Thai Cuisine" dishes formerly found only in the Grand Palace of Thailand. Equally majestic are the views from your dinner table: situated in an open-air two-story teak house, the restaurant offers sweeping, panoramic views of Patong and Kalim Bays.
Thailand, Phuket, www.baanrimpa.com

Mom Tri's Boathouse Wine & Grill

Scenically situated on the grand sweep of Kata Beach, the restaurant is also a port of call for sunset gazers nursing a sundowner cocktail. (Their sister restaurant Mom Tri's Kitchen is also popular.) *Kokranode Road, Kata Beach, +66 (0)7 633 0015-7, www.boathousephuket.com*

Black Ginger

The Indigo Pearl resort's iconic restaurant appears like a mirage of a traditional Thai wooden mansion afloat on a lily pond. What's intriguing about the menu is that all are local and difficult-to-find southern favorites. Be careful though, southern dishes are some of the hottest in the country. For something a little less thermonuclear, gorge yourself on the southern-style yellow curry with a fish fillet and veggies. *Nai Yang Beach and National Park, +66 (0)7 632 7006, www.indigo-pearl.com*

Mom Tri's Boathouse Wine & Grill

One of the island's strongholds for special occasions like birthday parties, this romantically atmospheric venue is a pearl in Phuket's fine dining scene. The prices are in the stratosphere, for sure, though the French and Thai degustation menus are reasonable enough without having wine with every course.

FREAKY FESTIVAL

The innocuous-sounding Vegetarian Festival gives the misleading impression that it could be some New Age gathering of vegans playing sitars, meditating and practicing yoga postures.

In fact, this is one of the most extreme festivals in all of Asia, especially on the last three days when spirit mediums become possessed by a pantheon of deities and pierce their faces with everything from hacksaws to chains and cymbal stands. They also walk on beds of burning coals and climb ladders runged with swords that could split open watermelons.

Held for nine days in late September or October on Phuket, this is the grisliest take on Taoist Lent in Asia. Most of the action happens at the Chinese temples and on the main streets of Phuket city, which is booked solid for months in advance.

Vegetarian Festival

Kan Eang@pier

Dine in semi-alfresco style right beside the pier on Chalong Bay with the satin-smooth sea breeze ruffling your hair. Choosing your seafood, whether it's a rock lobster or white snapper from the tanks out front, is one of those Phuket dining rituals that should not be missed. Classic Chinese-Thai cuisine is the order of the day, such as baked Phuket lobster or a mixed seafood basket. The complex's Baybar is tailor-made for pre-supper or last-call drinks, while K1 Kaffe offers American breakfasts, good coffee and karaoke in the evenings.

44/1 Viset Rd. Moo 5 Rawai (Chalong), +66 (0)7 628 1212

Siam Supper Club

For a taste of New York, Paris and London this world-class restaurant with a jazz soundtrack and black and white photos of 1950s and 1960s celebs on the walls, is just the meal ticket. The affable foreign owner describes the menu as "West Coast Cuisine", which translates into some palate-pleasing starters like "goat cheese salad" and mains like Grilled tenderloin of New Zealand spring lamb with roast garlic mashed potatoes". Though the pizzas are excellent too, and the famous "Supper Club Cheesecake" has ruined more than a few diets.

36, 38, 40 Lagoon Road, Thalang, +66 (0)7 627 0936, www.siamsupperclub.com

ISAAN BYTES

Of Thailand's regional cuisines, none is more popular or widespread than the northeastern variety. These Lao-style dishes are both savory and spicy.

Perhaps the most common is *som tam*, a kind of salad made with un-ripe slices of mango spiced together with tomato, chili, lime and fish sauce. Lao food virgins should try the variety with dried shrimps—*som tam thai*—rather than the fermented fish or the uncooked crabs, both of which will deflower taste buds.

Typical side dishes with the salad include grilled chicken (*gai yang*), "crying tiger" beef (*seua long hai*), sour and spicy *laap* (made with chicken, pork or catfish) and another tongue-tantalizing, meat-laden salad called *nam dok*.

Som tam with salted crab

THAILAND'S BEST SHOPPING
Shop until your bank account drops a few zeros

Chatuchak Market

For serial shoppers, Thailand is a gigantic bazaar. The country's culture and economics of disparity are revealed in your two main choices for conspicuous consumption and street-level survival: glitzy malls and gritty markets. Ideally, any shopping safari should include a combination of both; the street markets are full of local color and bargains, whereas the air-conditioned malls are retreats from the sweltering heat, with Cineplexes, food courts and family-oriented fun.

Another main difference is that you have to haggle over prices at the markets, but the malls have fixed prices. When bartering, it's a general rule of thumb to ask the price from the vendor, then offer them about 40–50 percent of that and try to meet in the middle.

Whatever your preference, from handsome handicrafts to homespun silk or designer clothes to computer software, you can shop until your bank balance drops a few zeros.

BANGKOK

Chatuchak Market
Also referred to as the Weekend Market or "JJ" in Thai slang, this is the Holy Grail for materialists and bazaar lovers in Southeast Asia, with some 15,000 vendors selling everything from rare reptiles to Communist kitsch and Thai exotica. The majority of the market, however, is dedicated to clothes and footwear. It's not the easiest place to navigate, and it's certainly not the bargain hunter's bonanza it used to be, but it's an essential visit nevertheless.

Khaosan Road
On Southeast Asia's main drag for backpackers, the street becomes a pedestrian only Mardi Gras for young travelers and Thai college kids every night of the week. Flanking both sides of the road are little stalls and shops selling fisherman's pants, beachwear, knock-off everything and countless knickknacks. Many young artists set up blankets and ad hoc kiosks for hawking clothes, curios and handicrafts too. It's a great place for party-hearty under 30 nightlife and people gawking as well.

Jewelry Trade Center
For all that gleams, the glitterati should take a shine to this 56-story colossus and its myriad shops selling the rubies, sapphires and other precious stones Thailand is famous for.
919/1 Silom Road

Jim Thompson Shop

The legendary promoter of Thai silk and the disappeared protagonist of an enduring murder mystery, has become an institution in Thailand and abroad with many sales outlets; just a look at the luxuriant silks resplendent in bright colors and intricate patterns will tell you why. Signature items include ties, handbags, scarves, children's clothing, T-shirts, cosmetic holders, cushion covers and fabrics. See their website for a list of other outlets in Bangkok.
9 Surawong Road, +66 (0)2 632 8100,
www.jimthompson.com

Pak Khlong Flower Market

Lotus Arts de Vivre

An outpost of originality in a globalizing world of consumerist conformity, the company's team of craftspeople in rural India, Burma and Indonesia are keeping the tradition of handcrafted *objets d'art* alive. Employing folkloric motifs and mascots like crocodiles, hornbills and elephants, these one-of-a-kind designs are crafted from coconut, rubies, gold and wood. After the Swiss-Thai von Bueren family started the company in Bangkok, they spread their wings to take connoisseurs on flights of fancy through their many outlets across the globe.
Thailand, Bangkok, www.lotusartsdevivre.com

Lotus Arts de Vivre

Pak Khlong Flower Market

This orgy of botany adds a lot of color to Chinatown's gray areas and deserts of concrete with roses, orchids, marigolds and all sorts of floral arrangements on sale at sidewalk shops and stalls.
Along Chakraphet Road near the
Memorial Bridge

Gaysorn Plaza

A veritable United Nations of luxury brands from all over, Gaysorn has a good selection of Thai fashion labels: Fly Now (funky haute couture), Senada Theory (Oriental-inspired fashion), Zenithorial (trendy women's and menswear), Myth (multi-brand lifestyle store), GGUB (vintage-style jewelry and leather accessories), Sretis (designer fashions) and Olivia Diamonds (upscale jewelry).
999 Ploenchit Road, +66 (0)2 656 1149,
www.gaysorn.com

Mansion 7

Community malls like K Village have been all the rage in Bangkok recently but, designed to look like a haunted house, Mansion 7 is the first "boutique thriller mall" in all of Asia. At the back is

Mansion 7

a real haunted house attraction that brings in hordes of teenagers every day (no kids under 13 allowed). Brought to you by the same masterminds who dreamed up the Plean Wan retro shopping village in Hua Hin, Mansion 7 only has Thai shops, including a magic store called Gimmick, a sex shop called Hidden Closet, and a few 1950s flashback diners and bars.
Ratchada Soi 14, www.themansion7.com

The Emporium

The presence of so many hip designer labels like Guess, Chaps and Esprit, as well as top Thai labels like Greyhound and Jaspal, make this an informal, multi-story catwalk for fashionistas. Book buffs will find fodder for thought at a Kinokuniya outlet and at Asia Books. Near the top is a Cineplex and a gourmet food court. The mall is connected to the Phrom Pong Skytrain Station.
622 Sukhumvit Soi 24, Bangkok 10110, +66 (0)2 269 1000, www.emporiumthailand.com

CHIANG MAI

Ban Tawai

Many of the goods on sale at the Night Bazaar and the Sunday Walking Street actually come from this village some 20 kilometers south of the city. There are hundreds of shops here specializing in Siamese art, hilltribe handicrafts and Lanna-style decor. For antique chairs and betel nut boxes, check out De Siam. For contemporary Thai furniture, hit DNK International. But there's also bronze-ware, ceramics, wood carvings, dolls, lacquerware and much more at the largest handicrafts village in the kingdom.
The Ban-Tawai Commercial and Tourism Information Center, 90 Moo 2, Ban Tawai Khun Khong, +66 (0)81 882 4882, www. ban-tawai.com

Central Airport Plaza

When you're burned out on shopping for arts and antiques in stuff markets, take an air-conditioned breather at this mall.

Bastioned around a Robinson department store, the mall has a wide array of international outlets like Body Shop, fast food franchises and a Cineplex. For silks and Lanna-style souvenirs without the bother of bargaining, go to the Northern Village complex on the second floor.
2 Mahidol Road, +66 (0)5 320 3640-59, www.robinson.co.th

Night Bazaar

The city's most popular after dark lure, the Night Bazaar is a helter-skelter arrangement of shopping arcades, street vendors, hole-in-the-wall shops, Akha vendors on legs, and tourists galore, all buzzing around the nucleus of the Galare Center. Some of the best buys are hilltribe arts, crafts and regalia, handwoven fabrics from the northeast, wood carvings, and shoulder bags with folkloric motifs. Most shops and stalls

are open 6 pm – 10.30 pm.
Along Chang Khlan Road, between Tha Phae Road and Si Donchai Road

Sunday Walking Street

The city's artsy and folky side reveals its true colors every Sunday from 5 pm to midnight with this carnival of conspicuous consumption crossed with a jamboree of buskers and other entertainers and a movable feast of meals and deals on wheels. Loads of little vendors set up shop around Tha Pae Gate and along Ratchadamnoen Road.

Thai Silk Village

Out on the so-called "Handicrafts Highway" of San Khampaeng Road, flanked by shops catering to package tourists descending in droves, vending lacquerware, celadon, wood carvings and hand-painted parasols at the Bo San

Thai silk

Village, the best deal going is silk. In business since 1991, this old standby stocks everything from table sets to neckties, women's wear, slippers, scarves and other perfect souvenirs or gifts.

120/11 Moo 3, Sanklang Chiangmai-Sankampaeng Road., Km 3, +66 (0)5 333 8357, (0)5 339 0223, www.thaisilkvillage

KO SAMUI

Beach Road

This is your one-stop shop on Samui, a long strip running down Chaweng where you'll find all the brand name shops, cheap beachwear stalls, Western pharmacies and specialty outlets like painters who will sell a replica Van Gogh for a few hundred bucks. You'll find a lot of the same stuff on Lamai and Bo Phut for much cheaper. But there are some original shops like Life's a Beach with Aussie beachwear, and Chandra, an exotic boutique with clothes, shoes and handbags.

Classic Gems

Buying gemstones can be dicey in Thailand, but at this gem of a shop where they supply a certificate of authenticity you don't have to gamble. All of these scintillating 14 and 18 karat pieces are hand-made, and the gems are cut and polished at their own factory. Romantics and would-be honeymooners take note: their specialty is wedding and engage-ment rings.

46/1-3 Ruck Samui Building, opposite the Central Samui Hotel on Chaweng Beach, +66 (0)7 723 0479

Naga Pearl Farm

Pearls are one of the few indigenous

souvenirs you'll find here. On the nearby island of Ko Matsum, the Naga Pearl Farm is a cultured delight for visitors interested in getting to know more about pearls and shoppers interested in pur-chasing necklaces and handicrafts from the gift shop. Many tour companies offer one-day package tours to visit the island and pearl farm.

The island is a 20-minute boat trip from Ban Thong Krut

Trend Fashion

Tailor shops are all over the touristy areas of Thailand. Generally speaking, the quality, fabrics and prices are simi-lar, though it does pay to shop around and bargain. Most of them will offer discounts for purchasing two suits or dresses and will throw in extras like shirts or ties. Trend Fashion over on Chaweng is a good bet. They offer all the latest styles from Gucci, Versace and Calvin Klein, and a good area of menswear and women's clothes too.

91 Moo 3 Chaweng Beach Road, +66 (0)7 742 2387, www.trendfashion.co.th

PHUKET

Central Festival Phuket

The island's biggest comfort zone for shoppers, this mall has a good selection of shops for women in search of clothes and/or beauty treatments up on the fourth floor, men of action (Camel, Lee and Manchester United have outlets on the second floor) and an "EDU Planet" learning center for kids on the second floor.

74-75 Moo 5 Vichitsongkram Road, Phuket city, +66 (0)7 628 1111, www.centralfesti-valphuket.com

Chai Batik

For a truly original keepsake or gift, make your way to the island's best batik shop, where these exuberantly colorful fabrics, T-shirts and fashion accessories have been made into wearable artworks by Chai, the Thai artist who runs the place.

16/3-4 Moo 3 Chaofa Road, +66 (0)7 621 4502

Chan's Antiques

For the past two decades, this has been the largest retailer of antiques on the island. More than 1,000 square meters of floor space has been given over to exquisite art, bronzeware and furniture from Thailand, Myanmar, Cambodia and Laos.

99/42 Moo 5, Chalermprakiat R.9 Rd, the Phuket City bypass road, +66 (0)7 626 1416, www.chans-antique.com

Island Furniture

To furnish your tropical dream home, or just that spare room back home, this is the island's best furniture and décor shop. Choose from teak and bamboo products that are covered with everything from water hyacinth to Thai silk. This is also a good launching pad for daydreams.

90/4 Moo 2 Chaofar West Road Vichit, outside Phuket city and 2.4 km south of Central Festival, www.islandfurniture-phuket.com

Island Furniture

THAILAND'S HIPPEST NIGHTSPOTS
No red lights in sight, only green and disco neon

Where once Thailand's nightlife was both loved and lamented for its bawdy, anything goes nature, it's now become an altogether more worldly affair with design savvy nightclubs, wine bars and mega-discos with international DJs.

BANGKOK

Hemingway's
The coolest and classiest new venue to pop in Bangkok is this renovated golden teak mansion from the '20s, just beside the Asoke BTS, which boasts a garden area and fountain, and other rooms and dishes inspired by the author's wanderings through Paris, Cuba and Florida. *1 Sukhumvit Soi 14, +66 2 653 3900, www. hemingwaysbangkok.com*

Iron Fairies
The most original bar in the city combines industrial chic, a metalworking shop, live jazz and gourmet burgers into a cosmopolitan combo. The owner is also the mastermind behind the nearby Fat Gutz. *395 Sukhumvit Soi 55, +66 (0)2 714 8875, www.theironfairies.com*

Long Table
This sibling of the once-popular/now-closed Bed Supperclub boasts the longest dining table on the planet. Like its bedfellow, the Long Table specializes in traditional Thai dishes with uniquely modern presentations.

Hemingway's

The ambience is equally ambitious, with a series of video art installations and a 25th floor lookout on Bangkok's neon nightscape.

48 Column Building, Sukhumvit Soi 16, +66 (0)2 302 2557 www.longtablebangkok.com

Phranakorn Bar

Close to Democracy Monument and Khaosan Road, this hidden gem is a Thai-style Bohemian bar that has an art gallery on the second floor and a pool table and bar on the third. Up on the roof is the *piece de resistance*: an open-air terrace with views of the illuminated Golden Mount. An excellent range of cocktails with boozer-friendly prices and an extensive Thai menu are other enticements.

58/2 Soi Damnoen Klang, just off Ratchadamnoen Klang Road, +66 (0)2 282 7507

Q Bar

A legendary dance club with local and imported spin doctors, Q Bar is also famous for its intoxicating selection of spirits, like 70 different brands of vodka. For chilling out, they have an alfresco terrace upstairs and a chic Japanese restaurant too.

34 Sukhumvit Soi 11, +66 (0)2 252 3274, www.qbarbangkok.com

Saxophone

For live blues, jazz, pop and midnight gigs every Friday with the country's best reggae band, T- Bone, Saxophone is a hard act to follow. It's got oodles of atmosphere and an upstairs where you can sit on Thai-style mats and eat a wide range of local and American fare. No cover charge.

3/8 Victory Monument, off the east side of Phayathai Road, +66 (0)2 246 5472, www.saxophonepub

CHIANG MAI

Darling Wine Pub

Because of the luxury tax, wine can be prohibitively expensive in Thailand. Not so at this laid-back bar, where they have an awesome selection of wines sourced independently. It's a gay-friendly bar that attracts a mixed clientele.

49/21 Huay Kaew Road, +66 (0)5 322 7427

The Pub

In business for more than four decades, Chiang Mai's oldest pub is versatile. Besides the cozy bar there's a restaurant in a tropical garden and even accommodations available. This gay-friendly venue also whips up a formidable Sunday roast.

189 Huay Kaew Road, +66 (0)5 321 1550, www.thepubchiangmai.com

Kalare Food Court

For a taste of Thai culture, from northern tunes and classical dances to the brutal ballet of Muay Thai, this places serves up plenty of bites, bouts and beverages. The music kicks off around 7.30 pm. Later on there are ladyboy cabaret shows. Located in the heart of the Night Bazaar, this is a good launching pad for a shopping spree or night on the town.

Mix Bar

Housed in the city's funkiest boutique hotel, the Dusit D2, this bar exudes youthful class and sophistication. The drinks list, heavy on cocktails, is intoxicatingly long. Located in the hotel lobby, it's a prime people watching spot too.

100 Chang Klan Road, +66 (0)5 399 9999

Silapa Thai Lounge & Bar

Silapa means "art" in Thai and that's a good introduction to this artfully refined venue in the Shangri-la Hotel. An impressive list of in-house cocktails complements the "Thaipas" menu of local snacks.

89/8 Chang Klan Road, +66 (0)5 325 3888, www.shangrila-com

Rachamankha

The bar and restaurant in this beautiful boutique hotel mesmerizes with its subtlety and an indoor and courtyard area. The wine list of both old and new world wines will whet your appetite too.

6 Rachamankha 9, +66 (0)5 390 4111-3, www.rachamankha.com

KO SAMUI

Ark Bar

Undulate to the waves and groovy house tunes with the sand between your toes at the three most famous beachside bars on the island. Barring an appearance by the Four Horsemen of the Apocalypse, the venue almost always exudes excitement and pheromones aplenty, especially during the "Wednesday Beach Party" and "Funky Friday Beach Party".

159/89, Moo 2, Chaweng +66 (0)7 796 1333, www.ark-bar.com

Karma Sutra

To get away from all the beach parties, dance tunes and commercial razzmatazz of Chaweng, hit this lovely low-key bar and restaurant right on the Bophut Pier in Fisherman's Village. This Chinese shophouse has been lovingly renovated and it's got good food as well.

Bophut Pier, +66 (0)7 742 5198

Q Bar

With an indoor lounge and outdoor seats boasting jaw-flooring views, an Electro Lounge with DJs spinning dance tunes,

and a special "Q Kid's Room" for parents who need a break, Q Bar covers all the bases in style.

147/57 Moo 2 Bophut, +66 (0)7 796 2420

Green Mango Soi

This is the epicenter of after dark entertainment on Chaweng. Down this little lane are numerous beer bars, go-go bars, a few bigger nightspots like the Green Mango Club, which gave the *soi* its name, and its sister act Sweet Soul. This lane has the advantage of hosting a cluster of nightspots all within stumbling distance of each other.

W Retreat

Crowning the roof of this funky new resort is the funked-up semi-alfresco Woobar, which boasts commanding views of the sea and star-spangled sky. Regular and spontaneous "Happenings", chilled-out tunes and imported mixologists guarantee a good time.

4/1 Moo 1 Tambol Maenam, +66 (0)7 791 5999

PHUKET

DiVine

This stylish organic restaurant also boasts a Wine Cellar that makes a fabulous start or end to an evening. The cellar is an intimate setting with some 700 bottles of new and old world wines and 50 different wines available by the glass. There's also loads of different cheeses and tapas.

120/1 Moo 7 Thepkasattri Road, Thalang, +66 (0)7 633 6000

Simon Cabaret

At some point, most visitors will take in a ladyboy cabaret show and Simon is in

Simon Cabaret

Stereo Lab

As Surin Beach continues to capitalize on its newfound popularity, the nightlife is posing a quieter alternative to Chaweng. This diverse nightspot has a wine cellar, a dance floor and DJ booth, a Moroccan lounge, a games room and beachfront chairs too.

14 Surin Beach, Srisoonthorn Road, +66 (0)89 218 0162, www.stereolabphuket.com

Vanilla Sky Bar & Lounge

Get more bling for your baht and live large at this elevated beach-view lounge and bar overlooking Kamala Bay that gives off an aura of Ibiza cool. Part of Cape Sienna Hotel Phuket, this lavish venue, with a stirring mix of original cocktails, bolsters the hotel's reputation as a romantic retreat.

18/40 Moo 6, Nakalay Road, Kamala, +66 (0)7 633 7300, www.capesienna.com

a league of his/her own. The shows are flamboyantly campy affairs, as the performers gyrate and lip-synch in a variety of glittering outfits. Some of the humor may be a bit bawdy, but kids are still welcome.

8 Sirirach Rd, Patong Beach, +66 (0)7 634 2011-5, www.phuket-simoncabaret.com

Vanilla Sky Bar & Lounge

THAILAND'S BEST SPORTING ACTIVITIES, HIKES & ECO-TRIPS

Take your pick from rock climbing, diving, birding, golfing and more

The sportsman or woman will have no problem working up a sweat and a flood of endorphins in the kingdom, where a wonderfully varied topography combines with affordability to guarantee a good and green time with loads of exhilarating fun.

SPORTING ACTIVITIES

Scuba Diving the Surin & Similan Islands off Phuket

As the underwater capital of Southeast Asia, Thailand harbors shoals and reefs of sunken treasures. The country's marine life is spectacular: angel fish, blacktip reef sharks, giant clams, great barracuda, manta rays, and the world's biggest fish—the gigantic yet gentle whale shark.

For the expert diver who craves even more immersion, there are "liveaboards" to outlying areas like the Similan Islands on boats with TV and air-con that can accommodate up to 20 divers. This nine-island archipelago in the Andaman Sea regularly surfaces on lists of the world's best dive spots. With sites like Stone-henge and Elephant Rock, and fish like jack tuna and dog-faced puffer fish, these psychedelic reefs are a mind-blowing theater of marine life.

Mountain Biking in the North

The man or woman of action in search of heart-pounding excitement is guaranteed plenty of peaks, hairpin turns and off-road adventures up north. **Chiang Mai** is the sport's big wheel in Thailand, with the spokes stretching all over the northern highlands.

A number of outfits, such as Mountain Biking Chiang Mai and Crank Adventures, provide a variety of excursions fit for all levels. Some of the multi-day packages are grueling marathons that include all sorts of exhilaration-added extras like rafting and rock climbing. But for the more casual cyclist eager to give mountain biking a spin, the companies also have one-day packages suited to children and families.

Golfing

With more than 260 courses, many designed by legends like Jack Nicklaus, Thailand leads the Asia Pacific pack in golf tourism.

Much of its reputation comes down to two driving forces: economy and diverse geography that lends itself to challenging courses with natural water hazards.

Another factor is accessibility. Dozens of world-class facilities are within a short drive of Bangkok. On the outskirts of the capital is the highly rated **Thai Country Club**. In the country's first seaside resort is the second oldest course, the **Royal Hua Hin**, which was designed by Scottish railway engineer A. O. Robins and opened in 1924. And close to Khao Yai National Park is the stunning new

Muay Thai Boxing Camp

Kirimaya Golf Club & Resort, designed by Jack Nicklaus around a mountainous backdrop.

Muay Thai

Thai-style kickboxing has become an international phenomena with gyms in more than 80 countries around the world. But if you want to study a millennium old martial art in the original school of hard knocks, there's no better place than the sport's ancestral home.

Muay Thai gyms and schools of hard knocks are making money foot over fist in Bangkok, Ko Pha-ngan, Pattaya and other spots around the country. They are increasingly popular with female travelers, some of whom are professional or amateur fighters, but many who are attracted to the sport's aesthetic simply want to learn about self-defense.

Be warned; at some of these boxing boot camps you will be living and training with real Muay Thai fighters.

Rock Climbing in Krabi Province

For the hardy adventurer in search of a natural high, Krabi province is hard to top. The cliffs around the peninsula of **Railay Bay** have been staked out with rock climbing routes galore, from the simplistic to sheer Spiderman territory.

It's not a dangerous sport, as ropes and safety precautions ensure that a fall only results in a few scrapes and bruises. All the rock climbing shops offer lessons so rookies can learn the ropes.

Best of all, the routes on these limestone crags are embellished with some stunning vistas of sea, surf and golden crescents of sand.

Big Game Fishing on Phuket

From *Moby Dick* to Hemmingway's *The Old Man and the Sea*, game fishing is the stuff of macho legend. For those Captain Ahabs among you, the seas around

Rock climbing in Krabi

Phuket are swimming with opportunities to hook some really big marlins, sailfish, barracudas and tuna, or to do some nighttime fishing for sharks.

Some of the boats, like the *Dorado*, are licensed to carry 20 fishermen on day-trips, or sleep six on multi-day charters all over the Andaman Sea. They have a large selection of tackle, rods and reels, a massive non-slip deck and an Australian fighting chair.

Whitewater Rafting

The seasonal rains and lightning storms that put a damper on some outdoor activities from May to October only enhance whitewater rafting as the rivers surge, swell and run rabid from their mouths. For the dedicated rafter or kayaker, the rains add an element of danger to their white-knuckle adventures, turning a voyage into a rush of endorphins.

Close to Bangkok, and ideal for weekend getaways, the **Nakhon Nayok River** is a wellspring for this popular sport. The river is good for both beginners and intermediates.

But if you really want to go off the deep end, the northern province of Nan has become an adventure capital, with the **Nam Wa River** boasting rapids, small falls, rocky obstacles and "sweepers" (S-shaped turns in the river).

HOMESTAYS AND AGRO-TOURISM

As many travelers yearn for more "boutique" experiences on the road and getting off the beaten path, they are searching for holidays that give them insights into the local culture that they'll never get from a guidebook and meaningful trips that allow them to interact more with the locals. For these reasons,

voluntourism and its different facets such as homestays and agro-tourism are becoming big deals in Thailand.

Learn how to make a red ant egg salad. See a temple fair in a rural community and get a few impromptu dancing lessons in *ramwong*. Tour the local markets. Have your fortune told by a Buddhist monk. Stay with a host family and learn how Thais really live, work, play and eat.

Maybe you'll lend a helping hand with the rice harvest and drive the "iron buffalo". Maybe you'll help to build houses for the less fortunate or apprentice with a silk-weaving artisan or a Thai cook. Perhaps you'd like to be a Buddhist monk for a week or an English teacher. All over the country, homestays and voluntourist programs have sprouted up.

ECO ADVENTURES

Hiking in Kaeng Krachan National Park

Thailand's largest national park measures almost 3,000 square kilometers. It's crisscrossed with trekking trails that wind up, down, past and around scenery

Kaeng Krachan National Park

so green and pristine it might seem like a tropical mirage: limestone cliffs pocked with caves, two wide rivers (the Phetchaburi and Pranburi), grasslands, waterfalls and dense forests that are home to a wild array of species. Bear in mind that you must arrange your own transport to the park and that the rainy season from May to October makes most hikes a washout.

Bird Watching on Doi Suthep

Chiang Mai's most prominent landmark, Doi Suthep, is also one of the country's best nests for birders. Around 300 species flit through these forests, including sub-mountain species like the wedge-tailed green pigeon and the spot-throated babbler as well as rare winter migrants from northern Asia, such as the grey-winged blackbird and the sulfur-breasted leaf warbler. But this verdant mountain is also a roost for much bigger birds of prey like the black eagle and crested honey buzzard. Companies like Thailand Bird Watching offer full daytrips with an English-speaking bird spotter and guide.

Cycling in Sukhothai

No form of transport is more carbon neutral than cycling. Likewise, no form of travel is better suited to discovering the historical park of Sukhothai, the country's first kingdom. This time capsule of Siamese history is made both magical and mystical with the presence of so many age-defying temples, palaces, Buddha images and pagodas. What separates Sukhothai from the Khmer ruins in the country and Ayutthaya is that the first capital was never sacked by a foreign power. At certain times, and at certain places, this park evokes a sense of time travel—of being time-warped

back some seven centuries to a place whose Thai names translates as the "Dawn of Happiness". Spread over 70 kilometers, this UNESCO World Heritage Site is one of Southeast Asia's most magnificent historical attractions.

Diving in Ko Tao

Coral reefs, the so-called "rainforests of the sea", are the second most productive ecosystems on earth. The main difference between them is that you can't get a close-up on the rainforest canopy to see all the action and dramas playing out there like you can as a scuba diver swimming past a color-saturated reef. Learning to dive is almost like discovering a sixth sense, an extra limb, and a different form of deep breathing that is part yoga and part meditation. Not everyone is fortunate enough to become mermaids and mermen, but the gentle currents around Ko Tao, and shoals dive schools, have made the island the number one place for rookie divers to get certified in Southeast Asia.

Chumpon Reef, Ko Tao

THAILAND'S KID-FRIENDLY ACTIVITIES

Families flock to theme parks, cultural shows, zoos and go-kart tracks

The kingdom's accent on family values and all-ages attractions means that a significant number of visitors are families. Apart from the infrastructure and the lack of crime, Thailand boasts a lot of activities that appeal to younger visitors.

Angthong National Marine Park
Even the most hyperactive, easily bored kid will have enough to keep himself occupied on a daytrip to this impeccable archipelago near Ko Samui. Almost the full gamut of marine sports, like snorkeling, swimming and kayaking are on offer.

ATV Tours in Phuket
The emerald isle's topography of hills, jungle, beaches and trails skirting plantations is ideal for these all-terrain vehicles suitable for all ages. Even better, you can combine the tours with elephant treks and kayaking.

Crocodile Farm
For the heart-stopping finale of the crocodile show, the Thai star runs and then slides on his belly towards the reptile's open jaws. Stopping just in front of it, he spits a Thai banknote into the man-eater's mouth, shoves his hand into the jaws of death, retrieves the money and gives his co-star a kiss right on its ugly snout, while the crowd goes ballistic with applause.

Besides the shows and thousands of crocs on display, the zoo on the premises has a sizable collection of exotic birds (Indian peafowl and Australian cassowary), mammals (hog deer and Malayan sun

Angthong National Marine Park

Dream World

bears), as well as serpents (golden Thai pythons), plus there's some coin-operated rides for smaller kids and air rifles for adolescents to blow off some angst and hyperactivity.

555 Moo 7, Taiban Road, Tambon Taiban, near Kilometer 30 on Sukhumvit Highway, +66 (0)2 703 4891-5

Dream World

This amusement park in the boondocks of Bangkok is a miniature Disneyland. In total, there are more than 40 rides scattered across four sections.

The Dream Garden riffs on a theme of Mother Nature, featuring cable cars, the Seven Wonders of the World and the Water Tricycle. Fantasy Land revolves around renditions of classic fairy tales, most notably Sleeping Beauty's Castle. But the most diverse gamut of attractions is found in Adventure Land, with Grand Canyon, Bumper Boats and the deliciously spooky Haunted Mansion.

In the latter section, however, the biggest attraction is the Hollywood Action Show, a live spectacle starring a SWAT team taking on a group of terrorists.

On weekdays, the show bursts into shell-shocking action at 2.30 pm, although there are three performances on weekends and national holidays at 12.30 pm, 2.30 pm and 4.30 pm.

62 Moo 1, Rangsit Nakorn Nayok Road, Pathum Thani, +66 (0)2 533 1152

Dusit Zoo

The walls that surround the zoo are adorned with colorful paintings, along with the English names of the many different creatures incarcerated here: Asiatic jackals, scarlet macaws, leopards, lions, white-cheeked gibbons, golden Thai pythons, pygmy hippos, hornbills and blue magpies.

Originally, these grounds were part of the Royal Dusit Garden Palace and King Rama V used it as his private botanical garden. In 1938, Rama VII approved the government's plan to turn it into a zoo. Covering a total of 14 hectares, two-thirds of which is land, the zoo has around 288 different species of mammals, 1,018 bird species and almost 300 different kinds of reptiles.

71 Rama V Road, +66 (0)2 281 2000

Night Safari

A whole new school of future veterinarians and animal lovers may be spawned by relishing some wild times with lions, tigers, bears, and the thrill of hand feeding giraffe, zebra and antelope. But this Chiang Mai attraction is much more than a safari. After making a foot powered walk around the animal enclosures engulfing the lake and then doing the tram ride through the "open zoo", there is also a light-and-fountain show for a grand finale.

Ratchaphruek Road, Doi Suthep-Pui National Park, +66 (0)5 399 9050

Phuket Fantasea

This theme park is the best night out for families on the island. Take a stroll around the Carnival Village with special shows and Hanuman's Lair with games for kids before enjoying a buffet dinner in the two Thai-themed restaurants as an appetizer for the main course: a 75-minute spectacular that is one part circus, one part edutainment, and all parts Thai cultural experience, with elephants in battle regalia and a Siamese twins comedy duo.

Book tickets online at www.phuketfantasea.com

Phuket Fantasea

Siam Ocean World

Samui Go-Kart

One of those quintessential holiday experiences, go-karting adds a welcome dose of pedal-to-the-metal fun to a sojourn in the sun when laid-back becomes comatose. The three different sizes of go-karts here give all family members a chance to move into the fast lane for some contests of sibling rivalry and a change of pace.

Moo 1, 4169 Ring Road, Bo Phut, +66 (0)7 742 5097

Siam Ocean World

Southeast Asia's largest aquarium epitomizes edutainment. Every day there are feeding shows for sharks, eagle rays and otters. Even better for curious kids are the special contact shows with a rotating cast of creatures like hedgehogs, snakes, tortoises and amphibians. Truth be told, the glass tunnel where visitors walk through an underwater world full of the world's most exotic, and just plain weird marine creatures, casts a spell over adults too.

In the basement of Siam Paragon, 991 Rama I Road, www.siamoceanworld.co.th

Siam Niramit

Fancy a primer on the history of Thailand reenacted with the pizzazz of a Vegas show in a luxurious 2,000-seat theater in

Siam Niramit

Bangkok? Then Siam Niramit (Magic Siam) in Bangkok is the perfect platform for your fantasies.

These nightly extravaganzas also contain a trip into the heavenly and hellish realms of Thai mythology using special FX and flying angels, in addition to a roundup of Thai festivals—with audience participation and all due pageantry—from the four corners of the kingdom.

Also included with your ticket are a buffet dinner and a chance for a shopping spree in the handicrafts zone of the Village of the Four Regions. At the end of 2011, a new Siam Niramit opened on Phuket.

19 Tiamruammit Road, +66 (0)2 649 9222, www.siamniramit.com

Siam Park City

Amusement parks like this one are godsends for the young and the young at heart. Most impressive is the Siam Lagoon, with the world's largest wave pool, as certified by the *Guinness Book of Records*, at 13,000 square meters. What's more, the waterslide feeding it is three stories steep.

Many other adventures like Dinotopia lie in wait to capture fertile imaginations, as well as roller-coaster rides such as the Vortex to provide visceral chills.

+66 (0)2 919 7200, www.siamparkcity.com

Thai Family Values

In Thailand, where even waiters and waitresses are referred to as *phi* (elder) or *nong* (younger), just as children or siblings are, family-first values reign supreme, and this shows up in every aspect of their lives. That makes the country perfect for family getaways. The fact that Thais are continually fussing over children, and even standing up to give them seats on the bus or subway, means that everyone will be looking out for your kids. Eliminating such safety concerns from any parent's burden of worries will make for a much more stress- and strife-free vacation in a country where there is very little crime against tourists.

In Thailand, the second Saturday of every January is Children's Day. On this day, many institutions, like Government House and the Royal Thai Air Force, open their doors to kids, giving free tours of the prime minister's office and fighter planes. The Dusit Zoo also gives free admission to children, and amusement parks offer all sorts of specials.

THAILAND'S BEST TEMPLES & MUSEUMS

In this bastion of Buddhism, temples loom large

Few countries boast as many temples, shrines and testimonies to the spirit wrought in stone, wood and brick than Thailand. In such a dauntingly long list of architectural glories, it's difficult to narrow the choices down to a chosen dozen without missing a crucial few.

Though the country's museums are considerably less omnipotent than the temples, to really come to grips with its centuries of war and peace, its triumphs and calamities, its politics and culture, paying a visit to some of these repositories pays off by adding multiple dimensions to an itinerary.

AYUTTHAYA

Wat Pra Sri San Phet

In AD 1350, the capital of a soon-to-be-formidable empire was founded by King Ramathibodi I. His ashes are interred in one of the three massive *chedi* at Wat Pra Sri San Phet, within the grounds of the royal palace. Constructed at the behest of Ramathibodi II to house the mortal dust of his father and brother, the *chedi* stand as monuments to filial devotion. This is the largest temple in Ayutthaya and close to many of the ancient kingdom's most time-honored sites. ***Historical Park, Ayutthaya***

BANGKOK

Royal Barges Museum

Eight of these adjective-defying water-craft are on display in this canalside museum, where the gilded barges still used today rest on steel girders just above the waterline. One of the most remarkable creations is the vessel created to honor the current king's golden

Wat Pra Sri San Phet

jubilee in 1996. On the prow sits a wooden image of the birdman deity Garuda; under him is the muzzle of a cannon.

Many of the long-tail boat tours of the canals of Bangkok Noi and Bangkok Yai include a stopover at the museum, though all the motorcycle taxi drivers at the ferry stop under the Phra Pinklao Bridge know its labyrinthine location.
80/1 Rimkhlong Bangkok Noi, Arun Amarin Road, +66 (0)2 424 0004

Wat Arun
Approaching the temple by boat is a memory forever tattooed on the minds of visitors as the main tower, rising some 80 meters into the skyline and surrounded by four smaller ones, comes into view. All the towers look like they've been plastered with broken plates and flower pots, while at the zenith of the central tower is a thunderbolt. In fact, all five towers were built of brick, then plastered with stucco before being encrusted with thousands of jagged pieces of

Wat Arun

many-hued Chinese porcelain. Missing out on this temple—or at least glimpsing it from a river taxi—would be like going to Paris and not seeing the Eiffel Tower.
34 Arun Amarin Road, +66 (0)2 891 1149, www.watarun.org

Rattanakosin Exhibition Hall
If running short on time, skip the dowdy National Museum by Sanam Luang and head for the city's newest and most high-tech homage to history. Spread over nine different rooms, these multimedia shows illuminate the area's history, the legend of the Emerald Buddha and Siamese performing arts, and make a good point of departure for exploring all the temples nearby.
100 Ratchdamneon Klang Road, +66 (0)2 621 0044, www.nitasrattanakosin.com

Jim Thompson House
The house belonging to the so-called "Silk King" who mysteriously disappeared in Malaysia in 1967 ranks second to the Temple of the Emerald Buddha as Bangkok's most crowd-pulling tourist distraction. The six teak houses, surrounded by rain trees and golden bamboo, where he once lived and held lavish parties, are attractions in themselves, but the way Thompson furnished and decorated them with priceless fabrics and timeless antiquities is genius. Under the dining room wing of the house is one of the oldest Buddha images to be found anywhere in the world.
6 Soi Kasemsan 2, Rama I Road, +66 (0)2 216 7368, www.jimthompsonhouse.com

Wimanmek Mansion
On the grounds of this park and multi-museum compound, full of greenery, canals and bird-of-paradise flowers, sits the magnificent golden teak Wimanmek

Wimanmek Mansion

Mansion, King Bhumibol's Photographic Museums 1 and 2, the Support Museum, which houses a scintillating collection of Thai arts and handicrafts, as well as the Royal Carriage Museum, the Old Clock Museum and the Royal Family Museum. Paying a visit to what is also known as Dusit Park is one of the best (and most budget-friendly) days out to be had in the capital. (Save your ticket stub from the Grand Palace and admission is free.) *139/2 Ratchawithi Road, on the grounds of Dusit Park, +66 (0)2 281 1569, (0)2 628 6300-9, www.vimanmek.com*

Forensic Medicine Museum

The ghoul next door or *CSI* fan wanting to bone up on grisly exhibits of murder weapons, diseased organs, skulls and autopsy photos should not miss this house of chills, where the *coup de grace* is the preserved corpse of Thailand's most notorious serial slayer.

Situated on the grounds of Bangkok's oldest hospital, Siriraj, the forensic museum is part of the "Siriraj 6", a series of museums detailing anatomy, parasites, natural history and other ghastly subjects. The easiest way to get there is by taking the river taxi to the Phranok Pier on the west bank of the Chao Phraya River. *Adulyadejvikrom Building, Block 28, Forensic Medicine Building, Siriraj Hospital, +66 (0)2 419 7000 Ext. 6363*

BURI RAM

Phnom Ruang Historical Park

At the apex of the 200-meter-high extinct volcano Phnom Ruang is the temple **Wat Khao Phanom Ruang**. Gazing at the countryside below from this vantage point will leave no doubt as to why the temple held such strategic significance for the Khmer commanders of eight centuries ago.

Dedicated to the Hindu god Shiva, the temple contains a replica of his sacred phallus, which is a touchstone for reverence at all such shrines. One of the *prang* (towers) dates from the 10th century, while many of the laterite buildings and the pavilion called the Elephant Walkway date to the 13th century. *50 kilometers from Buri Ram via Highway No. 218 or 219*

CHIANG MAI

Wat Chedi Luang

This atmospheric temple still plays a pivotal part in ceremonies signaling the beginning and end of Buddhist Lent, as well as royally sponsored cremations. In 2006, the stupa where the country's most sacred image, the Emerald Buddha,

Wat Chedi Luang

Wat Phra Singh

for and from whence the name came: "Phra" refers to a Buddha image or monk while "singh" (like the beer) means lion. It's in the Wihan Lai Kham.
At the end of Ratchadamnoen Road, just inside the Suan Dok Gate

Wat Lok Moli

Close to the Chang Phuak Gate in the old part of town, this temple boasts a 14th-century pedigree and a legacy as a bargaining chip between the Lanna kingdom and the Burmese invaders.

Of paramount importance is the tower of spiritual power in the back. The castle-shaped pagoda was constructed at the behest of King Tetklao whose ashes, ironically enough, are interred there after he was assassinated in 1545. This structure, along with the brick foundations of the ordination hall, are all that remain of the original temple.
Manee Nopparat Road, just west of Chang Phuak Gate

CHIANG RAI

Wat Rong Khun

Approaching this brilliantly all-white temple from the countryside gives one the impression of seeing a mirage, but it's real all right, though the surrealism carries over in the temple murals that feature images from movies like *The Matrix* and *Predator*, spaceships and Superman. The mastermind behind this ongoing project, which began in 1997 and is expected to be completed by 2070, is the highly regarded artist Chalermchai Kositpipat, whose penchant for incorporating Buddhist imagery with contemporary motifs in his paintings is the blueprint for this temple.
13 kilometers south of Chiang Rai city

used to be enshrined circa the mid-15th century, was restored to its former brick-scarred grandeur.

Wat Chiang Man

Chiang Mai's oldest temple was constructed in 1297. Its history is concurrent with the city. Constructed after a royal decree from founding monarch King Mangrai, the temple's oldest and most impressive part is the Chang Lom Pagoda. Buttressed by 15 elephants, the architectural style negotiates a truce between the Sri Lanka-influenced Sukhothai era or Burma during its Pagan-era glory days.
Off Ratchapakhinai Road in the northeast corner of the old city

Wat Phra Singh

The temple, in the western part of the old city center, is a paragon of Lanna style. Many of the smaller buildings are particularly outstanding. Off to one side of the hall is an elevated library with a beautifully sculpted base embellished with restored carvings.

Though plenty of upkeep has been done on the temple, it's in keeping with the original style. Also well worth a look is the image that the temple is famous

KO SAMUI

Big Buddha

Even visible from the air, Ko Samui's most lauded, photographed and visited landmark is the Big Buddha statue at **Wat Phra Yai**. It's the 12-meter-tall figurehead of a working temple that also draws local devotees to pray on a daily basis and celebrants for holy days in the Buddhist canon. Clustered around the bottom of the stairs are a number of souvenir stalls and smaller shrines. *Northeast of Samui on Route 4171 near the airport.*

PHUKET

Phuket Seashell Museum

The by-products of Mother Nature's handiwork are surreal distillations of sculptural art. Giant clams, fossils, golden pearls and Indian shanks both surprise and spellbind. Also on display are copies of masterpieces that utilize sea-shells like Botticelli's "Venus Rising from the Sea". For serial shoppers in search of eccentric souvenirs, all sorts of polished shells and items are on hand. *12/2 Moo 2, Viset Road, Rawai, Phuket, +66 (0)7 661 3666, www.phuketseashell.com*

Wat Chalong

The island's most ornate temple is also hallowed ground for the spirits of two dearly departed holy men, Luang Pho Chaem and Luang Pho Chuang. Not only did they heal the sick, but the two former abbots tended to the injured of both sides during the tin miners' uprising of 1876. Both of them are honored with statues in the sermon hall of this ornate temple, famous for all its Chinese divination practices. Their spirits are believed to deliver blessings to those who honor them. The temple's high point, however, is a 60-meter-tall pagoda holding a relic of the Lord Buddha from Sri Lanka. *From the Chalong traffic circle take bypass road Why 4021 for three kilometers and Wat Chalong is on the right*

Wat Chalong

SAMUT PRAKAN PROVINCE

Ancient City

Visiting this 98-hectare complex, known as **Mueang Boran**, which features downscaled replicas of all the major historical buildings of Thailand, is the slacker's way to take in the grand sweep of Thai history, from such early influences as the Khmer Empire, right up to 18th-century Bangkok. The imitations of the temples, monuments, and sculptures are laid out like a map of Thailand so they're easy to navigate.

Even though all the edifices and epitaphs are reproductions, the painstaking attention to detail is such that even historians could be fooled by the stupendous stupa of Phra Maha That from the southern province of Nakhon Si Thammarat or the Temple of the Emerald Buddha.

Really seeing this place requires half a day and can be combined with stopovers at the **Erawan Museum** and the **Crocodile Farm**, both of which are nearby. Altogether the program lists 109 different attractions, including royal barges afloat on one of the many lakes, a sculpture garden, the Anthropological Museum, and the Old Market Town where you can shop for Thai handicrafts on a street lined with traditional wooden houses.

Probably the best value for a tourist's baht around Bangkok, the Ancient City is blissfully devoid of visitors. Rent a bicycle to make the sightseeing a little speedier.
Kilometer 33 on the Sukhumwit Highway, Samut Prakan province, +66 (0)2 224 1057, or 226 1936

SUKHOTHAI

Wat Mahathat

When visitors enter the UNESCO-recognized World Heritage Site known as the **Historical Park of Sukhothai**, it's appropriate that Wat Mahathat is the first temple they see. For this was the heart and soul of that 13th-century kingdom. Even today it remains of its greatest treasure troves of Buddhist art and architecture.

Besides the main *vihara* and *ubosot*, there are more than 200 smaller *chedi*, reflecting both Khmer and Lanna influences. The main *chedi*, however, a soaring lotus-shaped tower, is believed to contain relics of the Buddha.

The Buddha images both great and small, sitting and standing, embody the graceful Sukhothai style of architecture that is seen today as a golden age.

Seeing Wat Mahathat is one of the highest points of visiting this historical park that contains more than 190 ruins spread over some 70 square kilometers. The best way to see the park is by renting a bicycle near the entrance.
Located 12 kilometers west of Bangkok. Open daily 8.30 am–4.30 pm, +66 (0)5 561 3241

Wat Mahathat

THAILAND'S BEST SPAS & HEALTH RETREATS

The reverberations of the wellness boom ripple across the country

Thailand is the fountainhead of the spa and wellness industry in Southeast Asia. No country boasts as many such facilities in all price ranges, whether it's a streetside traditional massage parlor or a five-star palace. Increased concern for overall health is a global trend, and more and more foreigners are visiting Thailand as a spa and wellness destination seeking health, relaxation and detoxification. The havens of good health and bastions of recuperation below are the crème de la crème of a long list.

Dahra Beauty & Spa

BANGKOK

Dahra Beauty & Spa

Dahra Beauty & Spa reminds us that smaller can sometimes be better and quite a bit cheaper than the spas in five-star hotels. Offering a diverse array of massages, scrubs, treatments and facials, this Thai-style facility is good for whatever minor aches and skin blotches ail you. Book online for special savings. *154/8-9 Silom Road, +66 (0)2 235 4811-2, www.dahra-spa.com*

Devarana Spa

All the finely wrought details such as 14th-century Thai-style arches, sumptuous "opium beds", tinkling fountains and piano concertos live up to the spa's Sanskrit name, a "Garden in Heaven". Offering a full gamut of treatments from the cosmetic to the therapeutic, the Devarana also has a variety of products for sale, like oil blends, soaps and skin cleansers and treatments for the hairier sex such as "Soothing Sea for Men". *Dusit Thani Bangkok, 946 Rama IV Road, +66 (0)2 636 3596, www.devaranaspa.com*

Spa Botanica

As one of Thailand's premier business hotels, the Sukhothai is a home away from home for many businessmen. In search of rejuvenation on the road and to put on a fresher face, they descend on the Spa Botanica's "Spa for Men" for special 45-minute treatments. Making the experience that much healthier and more holistic, guests can order from the "Slim-Down Menu" with organic vegetables and fresh fish as well as "Healing Drinks" that combat jetlag, the flu or hangovers. *The Sukhothai Hotel, 13/3 South Sathorn Road, +66 (0)2 344 8900, www.sukhothai. com/Spa*

Elemis

Forget all the Thai kitsch, angels and silk, the first spa by Elemis in Thailand is a watershed in design smarts. The all-white interior radiates vitality and the floor-to-ceiling windows are enhanced by views of the golf course and horse racing track of the Royal Bangkok Sports Club across the street. Further distinguishing this spa in the St. Regis Hotel is all the state-of-the-art equipment for liposuction, beanbag chairs for mothers-to-be, an Arabian cleansing ritual involving therapeutic mud and a detoxifying steam bath.
St. Regis Bangkok, 159 Thanon Ratchadamri, +66 (0)2 207 7777

TRIA Integrative Wellness Center

Quite possibly the most high-tech, multi-faceted wellness facility in Asia, TRIA aims to integrate treatments that heal the body, mind and spirit, utilizing both Western and Asian techniques. From detox and beauty treatments to acupuncture and weight loss programmes, TRIA's strength is its diversity. This is reflected in the staff, too, which boasts an Australian naturopath, a general surgeon formerly of the Royal Thai Air Force and a Chinese herbologist.
998 Rimklongsamsen Road, +66 (0)2 660 2602, www.triaintegrativewellness.com

KO SAMUI

Absolute Sanctuary

A combination of Moroccan-accented boutique resort and wellness enclave, Absolute is especially recommended for yoga holidays and detox programs. Many of the visitors are stressed-out urbanites in search of relaxation and rejuvenation. The personable service and cozy accommodations are other pluses. Even those

not staying here should visit the Love Kitchen, where fine dining meets organic produce, with homemade breads and "smart drinks" on the menu too.
88 Moo 5 Bophut, +66 (0)7 760 1190, www. absolutesanctuary.com

Banyan Tree Spa Samui

This five-star resort and spa is the epitome of elegance. Back in 1994, the Banyan Tree opened Asia's first Oriental-style spa on Phuket, so rest assured the treatments are top of the line and so are the prices. For full-on indulgence, "Banyan Day" is an eight-hour-long program designed to revive every millimeter of you. But the most innovative part of the spa is The Rainforest, complete with cutting-edge hydrothermal therapies and facilities.
99/9 Moo 4, Maret, Lamai, +66 (0)7 791 5333, www.banyantree.com/en/samui

Kamalaya Wellness Sanctuary

Give your health a booster shot with a stay at this upscale resort built around a cave once used by Buddhist monks as a meditation retreat. The seaside setting, the boulders, the palm trees and the private beach provide all the natural touches to aid and abet a week-long detox program or the Stress & Burnout program. But you can also create your own bespoke programme good for whatever ails you.
102/9 Moo 3, Laem Set Road, +66 (0)7 742 9800, www.kamalaya.com

Tamarind Springs

This day spa has been designed around the granite boulders and coconut groves close enough to hear the sea whispering. Prior to the massage treatments in open-air pavilions, guests are encouraged to drift between the herbal steam cave and the plunge pools. The forest spa also has villas, "yoga holidays" and a café serving healthy, mostly vegetarian dishes. Situated just off the main ring road between Chaweng and Lamai, the spa's back-to-nature means no cameras and no mobile phones.

205/7 Thong Takian, +66 (0)7 742 4221, (0)7 723 0571, www.tamarindsprings.com

CHIANG MAI

Dheva Spa

On the grounds of the Mandarin Oriental Dhara Devi is the lavish Dheva Spa, which continues the resort's motifs of a Mandalay Palace. Exceptionally well-trained staff give guests the royal treatment in 18 spacious suites. There's also a large aquatherapy area and a Spa Café and Spa Boutique with exclusive products on display.

51/4 Sankampaeng Road, +66 (0)5 388 9999, www.mandarinoriental.com/ chiangmai/spa

Cheeva Spa

This handsomely decorated spa offers a wonderful array of massages given by therapists with the Midas touch. The Thai Herbal Hot Compress massage also gives off a few whiffs of aromatherapy. The best value-for-money deals here are the longer packages that combine massages with wraps, scrubs and facials; they are about a third or a half of what you'd pay at the big hotels.

4/2 Hussadisewee Road, +66 (0)5 340 5129, www.cheevaspa.com/

Green Bamboo Massage

Unless you're on a money-laundering spree or celebrating the IPO of your own company, there's no reason to splash out huge amounts of money on spas if all you're interested in is a basic Thai massage. This place delivers the goods for less than 10 bucks an hour. Interesting deviations are the "Yoga Massage" and the "Royal Massage" and the "After Trekking Package". The eco-friendly materials used to build this center in an old Thai wooden house are also exemplary.

1 Moon Muang Road, Soi 1, +66 (0) 898 27 55 63, www.green-bamboo-massage.com

Oasis Spa Lanna

At this day spa you'll really feel like you're getting away from it all; time traveling back to the Lanna kingdom during its golden age for a full gamut of heavenly, hands-on experiences. Try the "Oasis Four Hand Massage" for maximum relaxation or for something completely exotic there's the four-handed "Golden Lanna Massage" which incorporates hot oil laden with flakes of purest gold.

4 Samlan Road, +66 (0)5 382 0111, www.oasisspa.net

Tao Garden Health Spa and Resort

Tao is one of the world's most ancient and revered systems of healing and wellness. The "7 Taoist Secrets of Longevity" underline all of the activities at this resort and wellness center that specializes in many different traditionally Chinese healing modalities, such as CNT (a detoxifying abdominal massage) taught by a Taoist master, and gives a variety of classes and workshops. To round out this stunning facility in the mountains outside Chiang Mai, the Dining Hall serves organic fare and the Pakua Clinic specializes in holistic medicine.

274 Moo 7, Luang Nua, Doi Saket, +66 (0)5 392 1200, www.tao-garden.com

HUA HIN

The Barai

A residential spa in the upper echelons of extravagance, the Barai has eight spa suites for overnight stays, which are part of the Hyatt Regency Hua Hin. The suites are marvelously well equipped with in-suite aromatherapy steam and milk baths. Included in the rate are complementary massage treatments. From the balcony you can watch the sun rise over the Gulf of Thailand and then start your day with yoga by the pool.
91 Hua Hin–Khao Takiap Road, +66 (0)3 252 1234, www.thebarai.com

Chiva-Som International Health Resort

For celebrities and the private jetset, Chiva-Som has assumed mythical status. As the pioneer of the destination spa concept, it's won all the big travel magazine awards. When guests check in they first meet with an advisor to plan what they want to achieve, be it weight loss, relieving stress, anger management or packing in the cigarettes. Besides 70 treatment rooms and the organic restaurant, there are 58 stylish rooms and suites offering panoramic views of the Gulf of Thailand.
73/4 Petchkasem Road, Hua Hin, +66 (0)3 253 6536, www.chivasom.com

PHUKET

Abbysan Yoga & Wellness Center

Offering some 25 different styles of yoga, Abbysan likes to say that they've captured the essence of yoga straight from the source of India. But these are not mere traditionalists. They like to take a contemporary approach that stretches

yoga and its practitioners in fascinating new directions. Known as Stott Pilates, this school incorporates "the modern concepts of core stability and neutral postural alignment—restoring the natural curves of the spine—as integral to developing total fitness," the director says. Also on offer are at their wellness center is Ayurveda and naturopathy.
123/22-23 Moo 5, Bang Tao Place, Srisoonthorn Road, +66 (0)7 630 4277, www.abbysan.com

Atmanjai Wellness Center

These fasting and detox programs can assist in everything from regulating high blood pressure to quitting drinking and smoking to simply looking better and younger. They are the specialty at this facility on Rawai Beach, where you're well out of temptation's way. Under Western management and with a supportive Thai staff, the center also offers a good range of rooms all with air-con and Wifi at the Friendship Beach Resort, so you don't have to suffer too much.
Friendship Beach Resort, 27/1 Soi Mittrapap, Wiset Road, Rawai, +66 814 125 652, www.atmanjai.com

Thanyapura Sports and Leisure Club

A brand new facility that just keeps expanding, Thanyapura is a new dimension in both wellness and education. Not only is this a Sports and Leisure Club, it also encapsulates the Phuket International Academy Day School for toddlers on up to teenagers and the Thanyapura Mind Center, which combines Western cognitive sciences with Asian meditative practices and yoga. When on holiday and in search of more visceral thrills than mental skills, the center offers an Olympian abundance of athletic endeavors, and much more, with state-of-the-art facilities.

Thanyapura 120/1 Moo 7, Thepkasattri Road, Thalang, +66 (0)7 633 6000, www.thanyapura.com

Paresa Spa

Perched on a clifftop overlooking Kamala Bay, along the strip that is touted as "Millionaire's Mile", it doesn't get anymore exclusive than this resort. The spa features some five treatment suites or you can opt for massages on your private balcony. This palace of pampering takes its medical, philosophical and olfactory cues from ancient Thai healing arts. The scent of lemongrass, jasmine and sandalwood complement the treatments beautifully. Guests can also opt for the so-called "world's first self-actuated wellness retreats" and "Natural Detox Retreats" for anywhere from three to 28 days.

49 Moo 6, Layi-Nakalay Road, Kamala, +66 (0)7 630 2000, www.paresaresorts.com

Six Senses Evason

Six Senses is a trailblazer in spas, environmental programs and eco-design smarts. They are firm believers in and practitioners of the SLOW ethos, meaning "Sustainable, Local, Organic, Wholesome". This outlet is another benchmark in diverse treatments and earthy style. From Asian therapies and facial treatments to body polishes and cocoons, as well as purification programmes, Six Senses will tune up those first five senses and make you feel your inner potential while they whisk you away on a sensual journey.

There is also a spa sala on the nearby Bon Island that is part of this five-star resort.

Evason Phuket & Bon Island, 100 Vised Road, Moo 2, Tambol Rawai, +66 (0)7 638 1010-7, www.sixsenses.com

MEDICAL TOURISM

A few years ago, the Thai Customs and Immigrations Department was going to add a box for "Dentistry" to the Reason for Visit part on the immigration form. Because dental care is so cheap in the kingdom— perhaps one-eighth of what it costs in bigger Western countries—many people come to Thailand to get their teeth done, before spending all the money they save on the dental treatments to go on holiday.

Besides dentistry, many patients come for major operations and cosmetic surgery, doing their recovery time on the beach.

In 2010, more than 1.4 million people—about 10 percent of the overall arrivals—came to Thailand for medical care. What's more, medical tourism has proven itself immune to economic downturns and the shortfalls in arrivals caused by natural and political disasters.

Some facilities, such as Phuket International Hospital and Bumrungrad International Hospital in Bangkok have multilingual staff and departments devoted to international patients.

In 2011, the Tourism Authority of Thailand started a new promotional drive to enhance Thailand's reputation as the "Global Center of Excellence for Medical Tourism". Part of the program is a new website that serves as a good source of information on the hospitals, clinics, spas and Thai traditional medical practitioners and their level of accreditation and standards.

www.thailandmedtourism.com

TRAVEL FACTS

This section will help to smooth over some speed bumps of bureaucracy and other potholes to make your journey as hassle-free as possible. To allay the most common fear of newcomers—that Thailand is a Third World nation rife with diseases and scams—we look at the excellent hospitals (insurance helps, they are not cheap) and security issues (crimes against visitors are rare but over the top in press coverage), among other concerns. In fact, the levels of safety, the relative ease of transport (third-class seats on the overnight train notwithstanding), and the access to high technology mean that Thailand is now a Second World country with many first-class perks and amenities for moneyed visitors.

Below: *Tuk tuk* taxi in central Bangkok.
Bottom: A long-tail boatman ferrying passengers on a snorkeling trip in the Andaman Sea.

Thailand's accessibility and its developed infrastructure in urban centers and the main destinations for visitors make it an ideal port of entry and base of action for any globetrotter looking to explore Southeast Asia.

In general, it's also a safe destination, with little in the way of serious crime targeting tourists. That said, vigilance should always be your watchword.

Like anywhere, Thailand does have its complexities, formalities and idiosyncrasies. This section will help to bring you up to speed with some of these aspects, answer crucial questions on visas and health concerns as well as help you to avoid faux pas.

Arriving

Citizens of the US, Canada, the UK, Italy, Japan and Korea, any different European countries and most nationals from the Asia-Pacific region who have valid passports are eligible for a free 30-day visa on arrival. Royal Thai embassies and consulates abroad also grant 60-day tourist visas and, with the right paperwork, business visas. For an additional fee of 1,900 baht, tourist visas can be extended in Bangkok for 30 days and then, if need be, for seven more days for an additional 1,900 baht at the Office of Immigration Bureau, Immigration 1, Government Center Building B, Chaeng Wattana Road Soi 7, +66 (0)2 141 9889, www.immigration.co.th

If you overstay your visa, the fine is 500 baht per day up to a maximum of 20,000 baht. If you only have a few days overstay, then it's easy enough to pay at the airport before you leave. For longer overstays, going to the Immigration Bureau with a flight ticket out of the country is the proper protocol.

Airports & Access

The main air hub is Suvarnabhumi International Airport, located in Samut Prakan province, which is about 30-60 minutes by car, depending on traffic, from downtown Bangkok. Formerly the city's main airport, Don Muang Airport, is used for intra-Thailand travel, mainly on low-cost airlines.

At Suvarnabhumi, there are car hires as well as minibus and chauffeur services. To save some money, look for the taxi queue outside the arrivals area, pay and get your slip at the desk, and proceed to the taxi queue. Do not go with any of the taxi touts.

In 2011, the airport express buses were terminated in favor of the Airport Link, a 29-kilometer high-speed rail line that runs from Suvarnabhumi International Airport to the Phayathai Station, which connects with the skytrain, in the center of Bangkok. The Express Line is a non-stop service that takes about 18 minutes and costs 150 baht. It cuts the cab fare and traveling time in half. For 15-45 baht, you can take the City Line, a rail service with eight stations. Note, however, that it's also used by many Thai commuters and

Suvarnabhumi International Airport

does become crowded during rush hours in the morning and after work. The lines run from 6 am to midnight. Trains depart every 15 minutes.

Arriving by Train

The only rail line from outside the country runs from Penang in Malaysia to the Hualamphong Railway Station in Bangkok. Just outside the railway station is the Hualamphong subway station. Or you can barter with a taxi or a *tuk-tuk* driver to get to your hotel.

Calendar of Main Events
January
CHILDREN'S DAY: Celebrated on the second Saturday of the month, Government House and the Royal Thai Air Force open their facilities to children for free guided tours. There is also free admission to Dusit Zoo and discounts at many different amusement parks.

February
CHINESE NEW YEAR: Head for Chinatown to see lion and dragon dances, and free concerts, street markets and traditional Chinese entertainment.

March
NATIONAL THAI ELEPHANT DAY: The creature that once took pride of place on Siam's flag and remains the national animal is feted every year on March 13 with special activities in the capital and across the country.

April
SONGKRAN: The Thai New Year is celebrated for three days in the middle of the month with water fights in the streets, the ceremonial washing of Buddha images and other traditional spectacles at temples.

May
VISAKA BUCHA (VESAK): The holiest of all Buddhist holy days, Visaka Bucha venerates the birth, enlightenment and death of the Buddha. Thai Buddhists visit temples and make merit.

June
PHI TA KHON (GHOSTS WITH HUMAN EYES): The sacred and profane tango during these festivities in the town of Dansai in Loei province as young men dressed as jungle spirits in colorful masks run amok through the streets waving massive phalluses while traditional dancers gyrate, monks congregate and old men dressed as ladyboys swill copious amounts of rice liquor. It's a big inebriated party held over a few days in homage to the Buddha's final incarnation.

July
KHAO PHANSA: One of the country's most magical sights is of devotees holding candles aloft as they circumnavigate temples across the country to stoke the celebrations for the start of the three-month rainy season retreat for monks and the Buddhist Lent.

August 12
HM THE QUEEN'S BIRTHDAY AND MOTHER'S DAY: Shrines festooned with fairy lights garnishing the Queen's portrait are on festive display at government offices and private companies across the country. For a free party with loads of modern and traditional entertainment, check out the shows in Sanam Luang at night.

September
BOAT RACES: As the rainy season reaches its highest tide, waterways become speedways as teams of boat racers vie for supremacy via paddle power.

Loy Krathong

October

THE END OF BUDDHIST LENT: As the monks leave their temples after the three-month rainy season retreat, the country and the capital play host to temple fairs and colorful festivals, including the fantastical Naga Fireball Festival, where the Serpent Lord of Buddhist lore is reputedly responsible for shooting hundreds of fireballs into the sky above the Mekong River around Nong Khai.

November

LOY KRATHONG: Held on a full moon night, this ancient festival sees Thais floating little banana leaf boats, laden with candles, incense and flowers in all the country's major and minor waterways, in tribute to the Water Goddess.

December 5

HM THE KING'S BIRTHDAY AND FATHER'S DAY: Shrines and altars to the world's longest reigning monarch are put up all over the city, beginning in November, to celebrate his birthday. The biggest celebrations and fireworks are in Sanam Luang.

Car Rentals

There are many inexpensive car hire companies around the touristy areas. Unlike some of the car and motorcycle rental shops on the islands, you usually have to show a valid driver's license and passport, too. As in the UK, driving is on the right-hand side of the road.

Climate

Bangkok is the hottest major city in the world with temperatures averaging around 28 °C (81 °F). It gets more torrid during the hot season from mid-February to mid-April, when the mercury rises to 40 °C (104 °F). During March, however, it often seems cooler because of

the *lom wow* ("kite winds") that herald the kite-flying season. The rainy season, from May through October, can be a misnomer, as there are many sunny days and sometimes only one big downpour per day—often in the early evenings. September and early October are the rainiest times of the year. The most congenial weather is during the cool season of November through January. Since global warming is playing havoc with weather patterns all over the world, the seasons have become harder to forecast.

Clothing

For entering many temples, you must wear proper trousers and shirts or blouses. Many of the city's bigger and classier nightclubs and restaurants deny entry to people wearing shorts and sandals.

Customs

Clearing Thai customs is easy and baggage checks are rare. Officially, you're allowed to bring in one liter of alcohol and 200 cigarettes or 250 grams of cigars or smoking tobacco. With other items, provided they are not prohibited like pornography, drugs and firearms, you can bring in a reasonable amount intended for personal use and not resale.

Driving
Since road accidents are the leading cause of death in Thailand, accounting for approximately two deaths every hour according to government statistics, driving in the capital is not recommended. Not only are the roads clogged with traffic, but Thai drivers are erratic and drunk driving is commonplace. On the islands, there are loads of motorcycle accidents involving foreigners. It's much safer to rent a car or pay extra for a driver too.

Electricity
The standard voltage throughout Thailand is 220 volts at 50 cycles per second. Many plugs are two-pronged and ungrounded, so remember to bring an adaptor and watch out for shocks.

Embassies, Consulates & High Commissions
Australia: 37 Sathorn Road
Tel: +66 (0)2 287 2680
Britain: 1030 Wittayu Road
Tel: +66 (0)2 305 8333
Cambodia: 185 Ratchadamri Road
Tel: +66 (0)2 254 6630
Canada: 15th floor Abdul Rahim Place, 990 Rama IV Road
Tel: +66 (0)2 636 0540
EU: 19th floor Kian Gawn House 11 141/1 Wittayu Road
Tel: +66 (0)2 255 9100
France: 35 Charoenkrung Road Soi 36
Tel: +66 (0)2 266 8250-6
Germany: 9 Sathorn Tai Road
Tel: +66 (0)2 287 9000
India: 46 Sukhumvit Soi 23
Tel: +66 (0)2 258 0300-6
Indonesia: 600-602 Phetchaburi Road
Tel: +66 (0)2 252 3135

Laos: 3 Ramkhamhaeng Road Soi 39
Tel: +66 (0)2 539 6679
Netherlands: 15 Soi Tonson
Tel: +66 (0)2 309 5200
New Zealand: 15th floor M Thai Tower, All Seasons Place, 87 Wittayu Road
Tel: +66 (0)2 254 2530-3
Singapore: 9th and 18th floor, Rajanakarn Building, 183 Sathorn Tai Road
Tel: +66 (0)2 286 2111
South Africa: 6th floor, Park Place, 231 Sarasin Road
Tel: +66 (0)2 253 8473
USA: 102-122 Wittayu Road
Tel: +66 (0)2 205 4000
Vietnam: 83/1 Wittayu Road
Tel: +66 (0)2 251 5836-8

Emergency Telephone Numbers
The police emergency line is 191; they can get you an ambulance. Call 199 for the fire brigade. The Tourist Police hotline is 1155 and the Tourist Service Center is at +66 (0)2 282 8129. Calling the hotlines is free within Thailand.

Etiquette & Taboos
Thais are very easy-going people, slow to anger and quick to forgive. In general, they do not expect foreigners to know or comply with all their manners and protocols.
  That said, there are a number of points of basic etiquette that are easy to learn and adhere to.
• Do not point your feet at people or at Buddha images.
• Do not insult the so-called "Triple Gems" of the country, monarchy and monkhood.
• Do not attempt to enter temples wearing shorts or revealing clothing.
• Do not lose your temper or throw any temper tantrums, which are always counter-productive around Thais and may, in extreme cases, provoke reprisals.

In the "Land of Smiles", a warmhearted grin and a chuckle goes a long way to smoothing over any hassles.

If you learn only three words of Thai, the evocative expression *mai pen rai* (meaning "no problem" or "you're welcome" or a dozen other things) speaks volumes about a tolerant, congenial culture.

Getting Around

To get around Bangkok, the skytrain (BTS) and the subway (MRT) are excellent. Taxis are also very inexpensive, and the starting fare on the meter of 35 baht has not risen since the late 1980s. In touristy areas, where cabbies gather, make sure they use the meter; some will quote you a high fixed price. If possible, carry the card with your hotel or guesthouse on it—and have the hotel write down the Thai name and address of where you're going—so the taxi driver doesn't get lost.

Tuk-tuk are okay for short distances but too noisy and noxious for longer trips. You will have to haggle over the fare with the driver, too. Sometimes they will quote you an extra cheap fare for seeing the more impressive sights in Bangkok, but along the way they will stop at gem shops and tailors. If you buy anything they get a commission.

During rush hours, the only way to

get anywhere quickly, other than the skytrain or subway, is by taking a motorcycle taxi. It pays to know how far you're going because you have to negotiate a fare with the driver.

Unless you speak Thai and know where you're going, public buses can be a nuisance and are often quite crowded. Most of the bus conductors, except on the touristy routes, speak very little English.

Health Facilities

All of the major hospitals have emergency wards, but make sure you have either cash or credit cards with you. The standard of health care is generally quite high in Bangkok, though you'll pay more for private hospitals because the standards are higher.

Since there is no emergency hotline for ambulances, try some of the bigger hospitals like the Bangkok Nursing Home, close to Silom Road, at (0)2 632 0550-60 or call the Bumrungrad International Hospital on Sukhumvit Soi 3 at (0)2 667 1000, both of which have ambulance services. Since these hospitals can cost a lot, having travel insurance is a wise idea.

Language

Around the tourist enclaves and major sights of the capital, and at the Hualamphong Railway Station and Suvarnabhumi Airport, English is spoken. The further you get off the beaten track, the more necessary it becomes to speak Thai or carry a phrase book.

Mobile Phones & the Internet

After China, the second largest exporter of computer hard drives is Thailand. That should give you a good idea of how hard-wired the country is for both 3G smartphones and high-speed Internet access.

Getting a Sim card, or buying additional credit, is as easy as finding a 7-11 outlet in Thailand.

Most of the bigger hotels—even in the more remote islands—offer free Wifi now, as do a growing number of pubs, restaurants and cafes. For those not carrying a laptop or smartphone, the touristy areas like Phuket's Patong Beach and Bangkok's Khaosan Road have plenty of Internet cafes.

Money Matters

The currency in Thailand is the baht. The bills come in denominations of 20, 50, 100, 500 and 1,000 baht. Currency exchange booths and banks which have this service are widespread in the bigger more touristy parts of the city. Banking hours are, in most cases, 9 am-3.30 pm.

Many ATMs accept international debit cards, where you can also get cash advances on your credit card 24 hours a day. This has made traveler's checks almost obsolete.

Opening Hours

Banks: Most banks are open 9.30 am-3.30 pm, Monday to Friday.
Businesses: These are usually open 9 am-5 pm, Monday to Friday, and often on Saturday too.
Government Offices: Usually open 9 am-4 pm, Monday to Friday.
Shops and Department Stores: Most malls and department stores are open 9 am-9 or 10 pm, seven days a week. Smaller shops tend to close earlier but are often open seven days a week as well.

Postal Services

Thai post offices located around the city are usually quite reliable. If you have a big package to send, air mail is expensive, however. In this case, sending the package by boat, which will take 1-3 months to arrive in Europe or North America, saves money. Most post offices also have a packing service and EMS, which is express mail. The Central Post Office is between Soi 32 and Soi 34 on Charoenkrung Road or call +66 (0)2 233 1050.

Recommended Reads

A Woman of Bangkok by Jack Reynolds. Finally reprinted in 2011 by Monsoon Books, this is the most seminal book of all the red-light reads on Bangkok. Beautifully evoking the capital during the 1950s, the novel's depiction of a gold-digging bar girl seducing and swindling a foreign suitor has spawned countless imitators.

Bizarre Thailand: Tales of Crime, Sex and Black Magic by Jim Algie. From the author of *Tuttle Travel Pack Thailand*, this guidebook to the country's dark and wonderfully warped side covers all the most macabre museums, weird attractions,

eccentric characters and the most notorious ghost stories.

Bangkok 8 by John Burdett. A nasty murder mystery full of tawdry details about the city's neon tenderloins, the novel is notable for its depiction of a Buddhist Thai-American cop grappling with spiritual and moral dilemmas.

The Beach by Alex Garland. Famously adapted into a so-so movie starring Leonardo DiCaprio shot on location in southern Thailand, Garland's backpacker epic examines the eternal quest to find a new Eden and undiscovered paradise only to watch it fall prey to human foibles and corruption.

Tone Deaf in Bangkok by Janet Brown. A rare book by an expat woman of travel-oriented essays detailing her life as a teacher, lover, shopper and all-round appreciator of all things Thai.

Very Thai by Philip Cornwel-Smith. A veteran expat author holds court on all the intricacies of Thai life, from putting pink napkins on tables to the origins of street food in Bangkok, the Japanese prototype of the *tuk-tuk* and why drinks are served in plastic bags.

Security
For the most part, Thailand is not danger-ous. The biggest crime perpetrated against travelers is by the thieves who slash bags open in crowded markets so stealthily that most people don't even know they've been robbed until later.

Getting taken to gem shops by *tuk-tuk* drivers or touts who lurk around big tourist sites, where they tell you that you can make a huge profit by buying and reselling gemstones in your homeland, is another well-known scam easy enough to avoid.

Female travelers on their own or in small groups or women going out on their own at night have little to fear, if they apply common sense to the situation and don't wander around late at night.

Telephone Numbers & Codes
Thailand's country code is 66, followed by an eight digit number beginning with two for land lines in Bangkok. When you're calling one of the numbers listed in this guide within the country, you must add 02, followed by the seven digit number.

Some important telephone numbers:
International Dialing Code: 001
Directory Assistance: 13
International Operator: 100

Tipping
Many of the bigger restaurants add 10 percent for service. Check the bill to see whether not they have deducted the ser-vice charge. If not, then a tip of 10–15 percent will suffice. In small restaurants and food stalls, tipping is not necessary. The staff in bigger bars and pubs will expect a small tip. This is up to your discretion, however.

On tours, if the guide has done a good job, travelers will give him or her a small tip at the end of the tour.

Tourist Offices
The Bangkok Tourist Division: tel: +66 (0)2 225 7610, www.bangkoktourist.com. Their office is right in the historic part of town at 17/1 Phra Arthit Road. It's a clearing-house of free maps and brochures about Bangkok and other parts of the country.

The Tourism Authority of Thailand: tel: +66 (0)2 250 5500, www.tourismthailand. org. Their main office is located at 1600 Phetburi Road, and has a lot of free infor-mation about tourism across the country.

INDEX

PHOTO CREDITS

Pages 32 Bottom middle left, 96: mgoka-lp/istock.com
Pages 32 Left; 39: Photo courtesy of Mandarin Oriental Hotel.
Page 34 Top: Amosnet/Dreamstime.com
Page 35: Himmelssturm/Dreamstime.com
Page 37: Ajichan/Dreamstime.com
Page 40: sopose/Shutterstock.com
Page 44: Tomxox/Dreamstime.com
Page 45: Nuttakit/Dreamstime.com
Page 46: Michelleliaw/Dreamstime.com
Page 48: thongchuea/Shutterstock.com
Page 49 Top: Sutichak/Dreamstime.com
Page 49 Bottom: Kessudap/Dreamstime.com
Page 50: Slava296/Shutterstock.com
Page 52: Slava296/Dreamstime.com
Pages 53, 54, 83, 92 top, 105: Leesniderphotoimages/Dreamstime.com
Page 56: Mcpics/Dreamstime.com
Page 58: Hydromet/Dreamstime.com
Page 59: Skynetphoto/Dreamstime.com
Page 62: Tanewpix/Dreamstime.com
Page 64: Pius Lee/Shutterstock.com
Page 65: Kobchaima/Dreamstime.com
Page 67: Baitong333/Dreastime.com
Page 68: Photo courtesy of the Tourism Authority of Thailand
Page 69 Left, right top: Photo courtesy of Mandarin Oriental Bangkok
Page 69 Right middle: Photo courtesy of Mandarin Oriental Chiang Mai
Pages 69 Right bottom, 100: Photo courtesy of Siam Niramit
Page 72 Left: Photo courtesy of Mandarin Oriental Bangkok
Page 72 Right: Photo courtesy St. Regis
Page 73: Photo courtesy of Mandarin Oriental Chiang Mai
Page 75: Photo courtesy of Kamalaya
Page 76: Photo courtesy of W Retreat
Page 78 Top: Photo courtesy of Napa on 26
Page 78 Bottom: Photo courtesy of Nahm

Page 79 Top: Photo courtesy of Soul Food Mahanakorn
Page 79 Bottom: Photo courtesy of The Riverside
Page 81 Top: Photo courtesy of Mom Tri's Boathouse Wine & Grill
Page 81 Bottom: Isaxar/Dreamstime.com
Page 82: Tae208/Dreamstime.com
Page 84 Top: Hackman/Depositphotos.com
Page 84 Bottom: Photo courtesy of Lotus Arts de Vivre
Page 85: Photo courtesy of Mansion 7
Page 86: Bryan Busovicki/Shutterstock.com
Page 87: Razumovskaya Marina Nikolaevna/Shutterstock.com
Page 88: Photo courtesy of Island Furniture
Page 89: Photo courtesy of Hemingway's
Page 92 Bottom: Photo courtesy of Cape Sienna Phuket
Page 94 Top: Captainlookchoob/Dreamstime.com
Page 94 Bottom: Davincidig/Depositphotos.com
Page 95: Supereagle/Dreamstime.com
Page 97: Arztsamui/Dreamstime.com
Page 98: Goncharov2006/Dreamstime.com
Page 99 Bottom: Preecha11/Dreamstime.com
Page 101: Khuntu/Dreamstime.com
Page 102: Samarttiw/Dreamstime.com
Page 103 Top: Rognar/Dreamstime.com
Page 103 Bottom: Jarun011/Dreamstime.com
Page 104: Petdcat/Dreamstime.com
Page 106: Lonelywalker/Dreamstime.com
Page 107: Photo courtesy of Dahra Beauty
Page 112 Above; back cover top far left: Charlieedward/Dreamstime
Page 113: Malexeum/Dreamstime.com
Page 115: Toa555/Dreamstime.com
Page 117: Mayangsari/Dreamstime.com

The Tuttle Story: 'Books to Span the East and West'

Many people are surprised to learn that the world's largest publisher of books on Asia had its humble beginnings in the tiny American state of Vermont. The company's founder, Charles E. Tuttle, belonged to a New England family steeped in publishing. Tuttle's father was a noted antiquarian dealer in Rutland, Vermont. Young Charles honed his knowledge of the trade working in the family bookstore, and later in the rare books section of Columbia University Library. His passion for beautiful books—old and new—never wavered throughout his long career as a bookseller and publisher.

After graduating from Harvard, Tuttle enlisted in the military and in 1945 was sent to Tokyo to work on General Douglas MacArthur's staff. He was tasked with helping to revive the Japanese publishing industry, which had been utterly devastated by the war. When his tour of duty was completed, he left the military, married a talented and beautiful singer, Reiko Chiba, and in 1948 began several successful business ventures.

To his astonishment, Tuttle discovered that postwar Tokyo was actually a book-lover's paradise. He befriended dealers in the Kanda district and began supplying rare Japanese editions to American libraries. He also imported American books to sell to the thousands of GIs stationed in Japan. By 1949, Tuttle's business was thriving, and he opened Tokyo's very first English-language bookstore in the Takashimaya Department Store in Ginza, to great success. Two years later, he began publishing books to fulfill the growing interest of foreigners in all things Asian.

Though a westerner, Tuttle was hugely instrumental in bringing a knowledge of Japan and Asia to a world hungry for information about the East. By the time of his death in 1993, he had published over 6,000 books on Asian culture, history and art—a legacy honored by Emperor Hirohito in 1983 with the "Order of the Sacred Treasure," the highest honor Japan can bestow upon a non-Japanese.

The Tuttle company today maintains an active backlist of some 1,500 titles, many of which have been continuously in print since the 1950s and 1960s—a great testament to Charles Tuttle's skill as a publisher. More than 60 years after its founding, Tuttle Publishing is more active today than at any time in its history, still inspired by Charles Tuttle's core mission—to publish fine books to span the East and West and provide a greater understanding of each.

Notes

Also available from Tuttle Publishing/Periplus Editions

www.tuttlepublishing.com

ISBN 978-0-7946-0750-0

ISBN 978-0-8048-4466-6

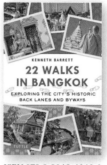

ISBN 978-0-8048-4343-0

ISBN 978-0-8048-4371-3

ISBN 978-0-7946-0093-8

ISBN 978-0-8048-4244-0

ISBN 978-0-7946-0627-5

ISBN 978-0-8048-4388-1

ISBN 978-0-8048-4390-4